Michael Legat was born in Londo[...]
School, Croydon. He joined th[...]
departments of The Bodley Head [...]
years' wartime service in the Navy
In 1952 he was appointed Editori
following which he held the san
Company. Since 1978 he has be[...]
lisher's consultant and lecturer. He has served on the manage-
ment committee of the Society of Authors, on the Literature
Advisory Panel of South East Arts, and as a director of the
Authors' Licensing and Collecting Society and the Copyright
Licensing Agency. He is married, and lives in Horsted Keynes.

WRITING FOR PLEASURE AND PROFIT

'Full of useful tips, and advice, about how to adopt a
professional attitude to the craft of writing.' *Publishing News*

'The most comprehensive and helpful guide to the business of
writing that has yet been published.' *Bedsitter*

'A comprehensive and practical guide to the business of
writing.' *Books in Scotland*

Also by Michael Legat, the companion volume,
AN AUTHOR'S GUIDE TO PUBLISHING

'A useful work of reference.' *Times Educational Supplement*

'There could be no more helpful guide.' *Daily Telegraph*

'Sensible and informative ... Mr Legat's book has to be
required reading.' *Observer*

'A useful, clear introduction.' *Writers' & Artists' Yearbook*

'Down-to-earth, sensible and comprehensive ... ought to be
studied by all aspiring authors.' *The Listener*

'Excellent.' *New Statesman*

'Invaluable reading for all authors – and not simply beginners
... we can thoroughly recommend his book as a balanced,
helpful and informative guide to the profession of
authorship.' *Society of Authors*

Writing for Pleasure and Profit

by

Michael Legat

ROBERT HALE · LONDON

© *Michael Legat 1986*
First published in Great Britain 1986
Paperback edition reprinted 1986, 1987, 1988,
1989, 1990, 1991 (twice) and 1992 (twice)
Second Revised Edition 1993
Reprinted 1994 (twice)
Reprinted 1995
Reprinted 1997

ISBN 0 7090 5261 8

Robert Hale Limited
Clerkenwell House
Clerkenwell Green
London EC1R 0HT

10

Printed in Great Britain by
St Edmundsbury Press Limited, Bury St Edmunds, Suffolk
Bound by WBC Book Manufacturers Limited
Bridgend, Mid-Glamorgan

Contents

Acknowledgements

The extracts from *Reader's Report* by Christopher Derrick, published by Victor Gollancz (Copyright © Christopher Derrick, 1969) are reprinted by permission of the author's agent, Anthony Sheil Associates Ltd.

The extract from *The Sprig of Broom* by Barbara Willard, published by Longman Young books and by Puffin Books (Copyright © Barbara Willard, 1971) is reprinted by permission of the author.

Foreword

Michael Legat, with over thirty years experience as writer and publisher, is the first to emphasize that writing talent can't be taught and that those totally without it will never make writers. But writing is also a craft, the exercise of skills and techniques, and here there is a great deal which the experienced teacher can offer. He can set out useful guidelines, warn against the commoner pitfalls, discuss the techniques and ploys which other successful writers have found useful, encourage, enthuse and inspire.

All this Michael Legat does with humour, humanity, modesty and with admirable clarity, stressing always that no rules are absolute and that the craft of writing can, in the end, be learned only by writing. It is his insistence that we must teach ourselves and work out our own salvation with diligence which is one of the most useful lessons in his book. *Writing for Pleasure and Profit* is the fruit of many years successful teaching and in its scope, undogmatic common sense and honesty is a worthy companion to Michael Legat's earlier manual, *An Author's Guide to Publishing*. Like that invaluable book, it will be of interest to the experienced writer as well as the beginner.

For Nancy
and for all my other writing friends
from whom I have borrowed
the best parts of this book

Introduction

There is a popular saying to the effect that everyone has a book in him (or her). For many years I have been cracking the little joke that in most cases it should stay there. It is perhaps a rather cheap laugh, and it certainly does not say what I really mean, which is that, though there may indeed be a book in everyone, most people have little idea of how to get it out of themselves and down on paper.

Writing is a craft. A few lucky people write naturally and effectively with little effort, but for most of us it is, like other crafts, something to be learnt, which is why the demand for 'Creative Writing' courses is nearly always high, and why so many Writers' Circles, attended mostly by aspiring rather than by published authors, flourish all over the world.

I must say, by the way, that I do not much care for the term 'Creative Writing'. It strikes me as pompous and, since writing is almost always an act of creation, as tautological too. I suppose it has come into use largely because those who organize evening classes need to distinguish between the composition of poetry and prose and the kind of writing which might better be called calligraphy. Whatever the reason, we seem to be stuck with it.

Some people seem to think that Creative Writing refers only to what might be termed imaginative writing, as opposed to anything which is basically factual and informational. But many who attend Creative Writing classes are interested in journalism or non-fiction books of various kinds, and those subjects, as well as the more imaginative forms, such as fiction, poetry and drama, will of course be covered in this book.

People who join Creative Writing classes usually do so in the expectation of being taught how to write – and are often disappointed. Writing may be a craft that has to be learnt, but it is virtually impossible to teach anyone how to do it. All a tutor can really do is to expound certain guidelines and to point out rules which are generally followed. If, however, he insists that those rules are absolute and inviolable, he is a fool and should be ignored. 'I was told on someone else's course that I *must* have dialogue on the first page,' one of my pupils said. What nonsense! I like to introduce dialogue at the very beginning of a novel or story, but it is *not* a rule that one should do so. The truth is that there are no rules in writing – or if there are, they are there merely to be broken. The value in noting their existence lies only in knowing what you are doing when you break them.

Writing is something you have to learn for yourself. All the teacher should do is suggest, advise, encourage. He can also, in a classroom situation, read the student's work and try to tell him what is good about it and what is less good. But the student must always remember that, although these opinions may come from a person he respects – someone of considerable experience, perhaps, with several published books to his name, and a good record of success with his pupils – they are still the opinions of one person only, and while the editor's decision may always be final, that of the tutor is not. Even if the entire class joins in telling you that this or that is bad or weak or wrong, take no notice if your writing heart tells you that it is the way you want it. You are the final arbiter of your work.

If it is difficult enough to teach Creative Writing in a class, it is even harder to do it in the form of a book, where the tutor is deprived of the opportunity of seeing and hearing what his student is attempting, and of discussing the work. So I do not set out to teach but simply to help you and to guide you as you learn the craft for yourself.

Some authors talk of the 'agony' of writing. I don't believe them. Writing is hard work (much harder than the general public believes), but it can also be immensely rewarding and enjoyable. However, it is certainly true that the more you put into anything, the more you get out of it, and the more you know about what you want to do, the easier it becomes, and the better you do it, the more pleasure you will get from it. I hope this book will help you to that end.

Please forgive me for using in most cases the masculine pronoun rather than writing continually 'he or she'. I mean no slight to women and ask you to understand that in all relevant cases I intend to refer to either sex.

M.L.

1

The Writer's Needs

Writing Materials

What do you need if you want to be a writer?

There are the obvious practical necessities, of course: a pen or pencil and paper. If you hope to be published, you will also have to have a typewriter, or access to one, though you could manage if you have a long-suffering typist friend who will transcribe your work for you, or you could pay to have it professionally typed (look out for advertisements in the small-ads columns).

If you type your own work, the costs of being a writer are small when compared with those of many other hobbies. Apart from the initial capital outlay on the typewriter, you will only need typing paper (bond for the top copy, bank for the carbons), typewriter ribbons and carbons. But large numbers of aspiring authors are remarkably mean about ribbons and carbons, and submit typescripts in a delicate shade of faint gray, and carbon copies which are virtually illegible because the carbon has been battered to death. It doesn't help your chances of acceptance if the editor has a physical struggle to read your work, so don't economize in these respects.

Many authors use a word processor nowadays. The cheap but excellent Amstrad 8256, which I use myself, is adequate for most authors' needs unless you want to go in for Desktop Publishing (supplying camera-ready copy so that the pages in the book will be reproduced exactly as you have presented them), when you will require something more elaborate. Most authors with words processors are addicted to them and say that they not only save time but actually improve their writing, because of the ease of making corrections, both as you write and afterwards when you come to revise.

Just as there are no rules about what and how you write, there are none concerning the physical act of putting words on paper. Write in the way that suits you. If you like to scribble in pencil, or work directly on to a typewriter, or use a word processor, if you want to write in an exercise book, or on the back of old letters, or on little pieces of paper about the size of a postcard (as Jane Austen used to do), please yourself.

Having decided that question, there are some other practical points to be considered. A place to write, for instance. Of course, you can write anywhere – in the train, on the kitchen table between doing the washing-up and preparing the next meal, in a book-lined study, or while lying on the beach at Torremolinos – but it really does help to have somewhere special for writing. Choose yours – experimenting until you find the place that suits you best – and stick to it.

Then there is the question of time. How many would-be authors lament that they would write if only they had the time? But if you want to do anything badly enough, you can make time for it. Get up earlier, or go to bed later, or ration your television watching and use the time you save to write. Even as short a daily period as ten or fifteen minutes, provided that it is regular, can be very productive.

I think it is possible to play tricks on one's mind in these matters. If you want to be an author, have a pen or pencil used for no other purpose, have a notebook which is exclusively for your work, have a chair that you sit on when you write, have a special time for writing; then say to yourself, 'This is my writing time, I am sitting in my writing chair, I have my writing pen and my writing pad – *and now I'm going to write!*' It is surprising how susceptible one can be to such an apparently foolish game, especially if you play it every day.

Getting the Habit

You will have gathered by now that I think the regularity of your writing is very important. Mary Wibberley, the immensely talented and successful romantic novelist, talks of 'the writing muscle in your mind'. Like all muscles, she says, if you use it often, it works well and painlessly; if you use it only occasionally, it is likely to grow stiff and awkward. Dorothea Brande, whose book *Becoming a Writer* is one of the best on the subject, similarly commends the idea of a daily stint, suggesting that, at least at first, you should not worry about the subject – write anything that comes into your head, regardless of whether it even makes sense, write about the weather or what you are going to do that day or how you feel about your family or politics or a TV show, or describe an incident which has stuck in your memory – just force yourself to put words on paper, get into the habit of writing, and you will find that it becomes second nature. Train yourself to write – the more often you do it, as in any other activity, the more proficient you will become.

Many beginners seem to think that writing is easy, something that anyone can do without any effort. Few crafts are as simple as that. If you want to be a good gardener, you have to learn about plants and how to treat them; if you want to make your own clothes, you have to learn how to get the hem straight and how to set the sleeves in; and the more gardening or dressmaking you do, the better you become at it.

It is the same with writing. The most successful authors are those who train themselves to write and work regularly to perfect their skills. Occasionally a genius comes along who knows it all by instinct and can simply sit down and write a masterpiece without ever thinking about how it should be done, but such people are very rare. Are you really one of them?

Writer's Block

This is the term that is used when for some reason or other an author feels unable to get on with whatever he is supposed to be writing. It seems to come in three varieties:

Firstly, there is the block caused by outside events, and especially by a major personal problem or tragedy. Serious anxieties over money, or perhaps a bereavement, can certainly smother the creative urge, and for writers who suffer in this way one can only sympathize and wish them a speedy release from their anxieties.

Secondly, writers are sometimes held up because some vital piece of their research is missing.

Thirdly, there is the kind of block which has no apparent cause.

Frankly, I have little sympathy with the second and third varieties. A very few cases may be of a genuinely endogenous nature, but writer's block has become a fashionable ailment, and it is certainly easier and more impressive to say that you are afflicted with it than to confess that you are lazy.

I am sure many writers truly believe in writer's block as a kind of illness from which they occasionally suffer, and would vehemently deny the slur of laziness. 'I sit down to write', they say, 'and nothing comes. I have tried all the well-known cures like doing something different which will take my mind off writing; I've tried to forget all about it for a week or more. But nothing works.' Perhaps the writing muscle has seized up and needs oiling. The late Norah Lofts used to say that her cure for this trouble was two very large zonks of gin, after which she would sit down and write with great ease; the resultant nonsense would be consigned to the wastepaper basket the next day, but the block would have disappeared. If that solution doesn't work for you, I can only suggest that you give yourself a very strict talking-to – tell yourself that you're a writer, and writers write, dammit – and then sit down and start writing. Ease the stiffness out of your writing muscle by going back to Dorothea Brande's advice, making no attempt to get on with the work that has got stuck, simply putting words on paper. Any words will do – that is the point of the Norah Lofts story, not the gin. Beaver away at anything that comes into your head until the writing habit has come back to you, and then the right words should gradually start to flow again.

A Writer's Qualities

Discipline. Perhaps this point has already been adequately covered, but it is worth emphasizing that a real writer, however well flexed his writing muscle may be, sometimes has to force himself to write. He may not feel in the mood, he may even be ill, but there in front of him is a blank sheet of paper (or the empty screen of a word processor), and somehow it just *has* to be filled with words.

Stamina. How many would-be authors have begun a novel and then abandoned it, sometimes after writing one chapter only, because they ran out of steam? Or got halfway through, and then gave up because what they were writing seemed boring, even to themselves? A writer must have the stamina to persevere through to the end of his work, to keep going even if he feels he has lost his sense of urgency, and to put up with the loneliness which is notoriously part of the writer's trade.

A love of words and a feeling for them. Good writers are fascinated by words, and their ability to express emotions, to describe events, to depict characters, to arouse interest, sympathy, anger or laughter in the reader, or to change his views – in short, to communicate. Good writers try to expand their vocabularies, are interested in the derivation of words, study their subtleties of meaning and find pleasure in choosing the most effective word in its particular context.

Imagination. I have often heard beginners say, 'My trouble is that I have no imagination.' I find it very hard to believe. Few people are totally lacking in imagination, and often what they really mean is that they don't know how to use the imaginative gifts they do possess. This is a failing that can be overcome, and some suggestions on how to do so will be given in later chapters on Planning and Characterization. Certainly, a writer does need imagination, but don't despair if you feel inadequate in this respect.

Experience. By this I mean experience of life, rather than writing experience. It is another requirement which worries some beginners, though the young, who may lack it, usually have enough self-confidence to sail ahead unperturbed. It does help if you know what you are writing about, and have been through the mill, but it is not essential. Indeed, if experience of life were all, books would be written only by octogenarians. We all have within us the seeds of humanity, and this fact provides us, I believe, with a kind of primitive knowledge which we can often draw upon to supply the lack of actual experience.

Observation. Writers are watchers. They observe other people's behaviour, they are curious, they analyse motives, they listen, they soak up atmosphere, and by doing all this they add vicariously to their own experience. Since understanding of others frequently begins with understanding of oneself, they also dig deep into their own souls and observe themselves with as much detachment as they can muster.

Something to say. This does not necessarily mean that the writer has a significant message to put across, but merely that he wants to communicate something, perhaps simply to tell a story. There is no necessity to be profound, but if you write without having something to say (except if you are doing it solely to keep your writing muscle flexed), your work will almost certainly be uninteresting, even to you.

Dissatisfaction. All good writers (and even a lot of bad ones) are dissatisfied with their work, always wishing they could rewrite it, conscious that they have not reached the perfection that they had in mind when they began, that they have failed to communicate exactly what they intended. Those with long memories yearn for the days when they could rewrite their books at proof stage (it is a curious fact, incidentally, than when you first see your work in print, all kinds of imperfections in the writing which were not visible in the typed version leap out at you), but since nowadays publishers frown on any but the most minor alterations on the proof, it is more than ever essential for writers to be self-critical before the final typescript is completed. More on this subject will be said in the chapter on Revision.

Self-confidence. While always ready to look at your work with a harshly critical eye, you must try never to doubt your own basic ability. You must always believe that you are doing something worthwhile, and that you have the power to do it.

Selfishness. This may seem an odd quality to include, but I do so because of the problem which I know faces many unpublished writers. The world reveres successful authors, but the amateur is frequently looked down upon, especially by his family, the members of which sneer at his aspirations, often resent the time that he spends at his writing, and feel no compunction at interrupting it. And no one who doesn't write believes that it could possibly be hard work, demanding concentration and perseverance. Therefore the writer has to be selfish, at least to the extent that he insists on having time for his writing, and freedom from interruptions, whatever the demands of family and friends. Insist on this, and you may find that some of the mockery will be replaced by a kind of respect, however grudging. If all else fails, build up a shell, a covering which will protect you so that you can simply ignore the outside world while you are writing.

A professional attitude. Are you one of those who say, 'I write a little,' and say it, what's more, with the self-deprecating modesty of a dabbler? Don't think like that. You may not be a professional in the sense that you make your living solely from writing, you may literally write only a little, scribbling the odd line now and then, but don't think of yourself as a dilettante. Say firmly, 'I'm a writer,' and believe it, and act like it, and be professional in your attitudes. Learn your craft, learn your trade, take pride not only in your work itself but in its presentation, take it seriously (which doesn't necessarily mean without a sense of humour). The more professional your approach, the more likely you are to achieve success.

I wonder which of the qualities I have listed you consider the most important. William Faulkner said, 'A writer needs three things, experience, observation, and imagination, any two of which, at times any one of which, can supply the lack of the others.' Perhaps those three, then, together or singly, outweigh the others. But I would also put a lot of emphasis on stamina and dissatisfaction.

Stamina, or perseverance, is desperately needed by writers, not only in order to complete the work that they do but thereafter in attempting to get it published. Never allow yourself to be discouraged by a rejection. If at first you don't succeed ...

As for dissatisfaction, it always strikes me that the main difference between the professional writer and the amateur (or, if you like, between success and failure in the craft) is that the latter is too easily satisfied with his own work. He puts something down on paper, tidies up a few words here and there, and that is that. The professional revises and revises and polishes and polishes, and when at last he feels that he has achieved something approaching the perfection he was seeking, he types the final draft, making still more little corrections and alterations, and as he sends the typescript to the publisher he does so with a sort of regret, knowing that the re-writing has to stop if deadlines are to be met, but still wondering whether he could make the work even better if he gave it one more going-over.

Writers are Readers

It should go without saying that anyone who wants to be a writer should spend a lot of his time in reading, and not just for pleasure. So much can be learnt from other authors' books, especially those who are accepted masters. See how they do things, study their technique, develop a critical faculty.

Dorothea Brande suggests that one should read a book twice: first for pleasure, and again, immediately after the previous reading, for the purpose of analysis. You can make yourself a list:

What did you like most in the book?

What did you like least?

What did you think of the author's style, his organization of his material, his plot, his characters?

What do you think the author's intentions were, and were they realized?

How did the author achieve tension?

To what extent did the author force you to use your own imagination?

Did the book move you, make you laugh, bore you, excite you?

Would you read it again?

If the book is non-fiction, you might also want to ask such questions as:

How did the author develop his argument?

Was the material clearly presented?

Did the author assume knowledge in the reader which he might not have?

These and other questions will not only increase your understanding and often your enjoyment of all that you read but almost certainly help you to improve your own writing.

Luck

There is usually an element of luck in success, whatever the field. It could be the luck of being in the right place at the right time. An author's success may depend on the chance of having written the right book at the right time and given it the right title and having sent it to the right publisher, and the publisher having given it the right jacket and brought it out in the right month, and so on and so on. Luck is undoubtedly important. But I also always think of that story about Moss Hart's mother when she was congratulated on her son's good luck in having three Broadway hits simultaneously. 'You're right,' she agreed. 'And you know, the funny thing is, the harder he works, the luckier he gets.'

Inspiration

You will notice that there has been no mention of inspiration in this chapter. Professional writers don't rely on inspiration. There may be occasional flashes of insight, sudden brilliant ideas, experiences which give a new urge to write or suggest a different and exciting approach, and writers seize on them gratefully. But that's not the way the bulk of the writing gets done.

When acquaintances say to me, 'I suppose you have to wait for inspiration,' I repeat to them my favourite quotation about writing which comes from the American humorist Peter de Vries. He said, 'I write when I'm inspired, and I see to it that I'm inspired at nine o'clock every morning.' That says all that needs to be said about inspiration, and about the professional attitude.

2

What Shall I Write About?

Why do you want to write?

If you are one of those beginners who say, 'I want to write, but I never know what to write about,' it may help to try to decide first *why* you want to write.

Perhaps you have in mind a record of some kind, a description of certain of your experiences, a memory-refresher, for yourself, for your family or even for strangers.

Or you may have something which you want to communicate to others because it interests *you*. It could be facts, it could be a story.

You might want to teach, which does not necessarily mean writing a textbook for use in schools. Think of the lessons pointed by satirical writing, or the way that Dickens exposed some of the social evils of his times, or the warning note struck by a book like George Orwell's *1984*.

You may want to illuminate some aspect of our world, to show it in a new light. This is one of the functions of poetry, but it can be done equally in prose.

Maybe you see writing as a challenge, something to stretch your mind in an effort to choose exactly the right words.

There are many, many reasons for wanting to write, including using the work as an escape from reality, or releasing your own emotions, or increasing your appreciation of other people's writings, or simply making it a way of talking to yourself.

And, of course, I have left out that most potent reason for writing: to make money. It isn't easy to earn enough from writing to live on, and only a handful of full-time authors can manage without a private income. Very few writers become bestsellers and rich. Nevertheless, there is nothing wrong in hoping to make money from your writing, and it is far from impossible to do so.

Choosing Your Subject

The standard advice is always to 'Write about what you know,' which you may find off-putting. 'I don't know anything. I'm not an expert.' Oh, but you are! You may not understand Greek, or be capable of splitting an atom, you have forgotten everything you ever learned about history or the parts of speech, you may have no comprehension of art or music, but you can consider yourself expert about your family and friends, the place where you live, your own activities, past and present. All these things are knowledge, and perhaps among them you can find something to write about.

Yes, but which?

Well, write about what you like, what you dislike, what interests you, what puzzles you, what makes you laugh, what makes you angry, the things that make you cry, the things that you love. Put down on paper everything that you would like to say but cannot for fear of offending someone, or of possibly looking a fool. And remember that, while it may be good advice to write about what you know, you can often find out things that you don't know, and increase your knowledge by observation, and use your imagination.

If you want to write fiction, you will certainly need to exercise your imagination, but you can still write about what you know. Choose as characters the kind of people that you know well, use a background which is familiar to you, and think of your own experiences in making up your story.

The novelist Frederick W. Nolan points out that most writers have a pet theme, which is the mainspring for all that they write; the idea first occurred to him when he realized that all his stories were concerned, sometimes directly, sometimes more loosely, with the main character's need for revenge. John Le Carré is on record as saying that the theme of all his books is the betrayal of love. I looked at my own novels and saw that they are always concerned with ambition. Perhaps by examining the books you enjoy and any writing you have already done, you will discover what your particular theme is, and this may help you to decide what to write.

Still baffled? Well, write about your children, or your pets, and their funny ways. Or try a piece on 'The Most Exciting Day of my Life', or take a leaf out of *The Reader's Digest* and describe 'The Most Unforgettable Character I've Ever Met'. If you stop and think for a few minutes, you will find that there is no end to the subjects you could choose – and all are things you know.

Some people find it easier to write if they are given a subject or perhaps a title. Many Writers' Circles like to prepare a programme which suggests a theme for each of their meetings; and when I am teaching Creative Writing I often find that my pupils prefer me to give them a subject for their work rather than to choose their own. You may feel that you too would respond more productively if you had someone to spur you on in that way. But in fact you don't need anyone else; you can do it for yourself. Take a noun, make it a title ('The Meeting', 'The Fan', 'Grass') and then set about writing a story, an article, a poem, to fit in. Or invent a first line (' "Good gracious!" said Miss Harris,' for example) and see where you go from there.

The one really important thing is to *care* about what you write. If you are personally involved in what you are writing, perhaps expressing your own deep feelings, if it is something you want to write, and not just as an exercise, not only will you find the writing easier but it will have that essential ring of sincerity and integrity.

Keeping a Diary

One of the best ways to begin writing is with a diary – the kind which you write at the end of the day, recording and commenting on what you did, what you have seen, perhaps what is happening in the world outside.

'Keep a diary,' said Mae West, 'and some day it'll keep you.' That may be true for the famous, but not for those of us who live a much more humdrum existence. Nevertheless, I think it is worth doing not only for the practice in writing that you get from it but because you will be producing something that you will enjoy re-reading in future years and which will be, I am sure, of enormous interest to your children and your children's children. However dull the entries might have been and trivial the events, I always wish that my parents and grandparents had kept diaries. Wouldn't you like to know what your forebears did and thought in the days of their youth, and indeed throughout their lives? If your parents are still living, perhaps you can persuade them to talk about the past so that you can record the details.

If the idea of a daily diary does not appeal to you, try at least writing one when you are on holiday, recording the places you visit and the unusual sights you see.

Even if you do not lead the life of a Mae West, it is possible that at some future date your diary might have a commercial value because the public is always interested in so-called 'nostalgia' books, which describe the bygone life-styles of quite ordinary people.

Writing for a Market

Another possibility is to look at what is actually published and attempt to write for an existing market. Nancy Martin, who had a very successful writing career stretching over fifty years or more, and was still busily writing well into her nineties, had much of her work published because she studied the market carefully and then decided, 'I could write such-and-such for *such-and-such a market*.'

True stories about three well-known writers, Claire Rayner, Mickey Spillane and J.T. Edson, illustrate variations on this theme.

Claire Rayner's immense success has been based largely on her versatility (and, of course, skill); she writes novels, in various genres, and non-fiction books on many different subjects, she is a journalist, an agony auntie, a radio and television personality, an educationalist, an entertainer. And she has done all this by watching what others do, and saying to herself, 'I could do that,' and then doing it – and often doing it better.

Mickey Spillane was employed as an editor in a publishing house which produced 'pulp' fiction. He looked at what he had read, and thought that he could do better. He wrote *I, the Jury* and immediately launched himself on a bestselling career.

J.T. Edson loved Westerns and read them voraciously. But none of the books he read really satisfied him. So he decided that he would write the kind of Western that he himself really wanted to read, and millions of copies of his books have been sold.

There is an important point in that last story. Always write primarily for yourself. You can write with an eye on a market, and certainly with the idea that other people will be reading your work, but never be untrue to yourself. You may think, for instance, that it will help your work to sell if you put in a lot of explicit sexual detail; that is fine, if you like writing that kind of material (and if you are good at it), but don't try it if it goes against the grain.

What Form Should Your Writing Take?

Some writers know instinctively what kind of writing will suit their abilities. Poets tend to be born and many of them, with certain notable exceptions, have little interest in any other genre; this certainly seems to be true of the poets of my acquaintance who belong to Writers' Circles or who come to Creative Writing courses. Others may, for instance, have a journalistic bent and turn instinctively to reports and articles; and there are natural historians and biographers and (especially if they are teachers) writers of textbooks. But most beginners do not have this certainty, and at the average Writers' Circle you will discover that the most popular form of writing is the short story.

I find this surprising, because the short story is one of the most difficult exercises that any writer can undertake. Short stories have to be written with great precision and control; because they are limited in length, their construction has to be tighter, and even their words must be more carefully chosen; since they are almost always focused on a single event and a small number of characters, they demand a strong narrative sense and rapid establishment of the situation and those involved in it; and there is neither the time nor the space to build up tension gradually – it has to be there from the start. Of course, most of that should apply to a full-length novel too, or to almost any kind of writing. But the novel does offer much greater scope and freedom, and I wish beginners would try their hands at a longer work instead of concentrating exclusively on short stories.

Of course, I understand very well why the short story seems so attractive. It can be written in a short space of time, perhaps even in one evening, and its limitations in the number of characters and events described may be seen as virtues. I often hear beginners say, 'Oh, I could never work out the plot of a novel – it's much too complicated a business for me. Besides, the thought of having to write fifty thousand words or more is just too daunting.' In the chapter on Planning I will try to help with the construction of a plot for a novel. As for the stamina required to write a book-length story, if you could manage to write every day one page of a school exercise book – say, 250 words (which is not very much) – by the end of a year you would have produced over 90,000 words (which would make a fairly long novel).

But I don't want to force anyone into writing novels if that is not their forte. Some writers are miniaturists and should stick to the short story. Besides, for a beginner the main thing is to practise your writing regularly, and if you find at first that the short story has a greater appeal for you, then there will be time later, when you have gained more experience, to move on to the novel.

On the other hand, there is no obligation to start with the short story, just because so many others do. Go in for a little self-analysis and find out how your mind works, and in what sort of shape ideas come to you – do you, for instance, see brief scenes which are complete in themselves, or do you find yourself beginning a longer exploration of a number of events and the people involved in them? Try to work out which of the various forms of writing would suit your ideas best.

Libel

If you write, as advised, about things (and people) you know, are you in danger of being sued for libel?

The first thing to note is that you can't libel anyone unless you say something about him which will damage him in the eyes of others. You are in no danger, therefore, until you describe someone in uncomplimentary terms or ascribe to them scandalous or criminal actions. You can also stop worrying about anyone who is dead, since the dead cannot legally be libelled, though if you say anything about a real-life person, now dead, which could reflect deleteriously on the morals or the physical condition of his descendants, it is possible that living members of the family could sue for libel on their own behalf.

If you do write unpleasant things about a living person, you will not be safe from libel unless he is totally unrecognizable in your book. To give a character drawn directly from life a different name, physical appearance, occupation and so on will not protect you if that person is still recognizable to his friends and acquaintances, and if you have maligned him. And it is no defence to put in the front of the book some statement to the effect that 'The characters in this book are fictitious, and any resemblance to actual persons, living or dead, is purely coincidental.'

If you can prove that what you have said about someone is true, that may be an adequate defence if he sues you. Nevertheless, you may be involved in considerable legal costs.

It is advisable not to draw directly from life any character to whom you are going to impute dishonesty or immorality of any kind. Invent such characters out of your imagination, and if you insist on using a model, alter everything about him that you possibly can.

If you are in any doubt about whether or not you have libelled someone in a work which has been accepted for publication, you have an obligation to tell the publisher of your worries. This will not necessarily mean that he will abandon plans for publication, but he will undoubtedly consider the problem carefully and advise you on it, and may ask you to make changes in the relevant passages.

Titles

Whatever kind of writing you do, a good title is worth trying to find. What you want is something simple, relevant and memorable, and preferably giving an indication of what type of book it is. If you can also make it somehow intriguing, so that it immediately arouses interest in the potential reader's mind and makes him want to know what the book or story is all about, that is a bonus.

Some writers have a great talent for finding titles, while others struggle over them. A well-known quotation is often used, but not nearly so often as in the past. But whatever you choose, be prepared for it to be changed later. Publishers, with some justification – not a lot, but some – consider themselves to be experts on the kind of titles that are successful, and may well discard the wording that you have laboured over for so long, and substitute something boring, or quite unsuitable, or both. How hard you fight on this matter depends largely on your relationship with your publisher.

Many writers have an obsessive need to fix a title before they actually begin writing, and become quite neurotic if they cannot find anything they like. I try to persuade such authors not to bother about it – the title is not really important while you are writing your story or article or play, and can be decided upon later. But if it really worries you, it is probably better advice to tell you to spend as much time as you need on the choice.

3

Planning

Synopses

Put a group of Creative Writing tutors together and they will agree on most subjects – but not about whether or not you should prepare a synopsis of your work before you begin to write it. Those who are not in favour say, 'Just write. To plan in advance in too much detail ruins spontaneity, encases your imagination in rigid confines, inhibits the natural development of what you are writing and makes for a contrived plot; in any case many writers just cannot work that way.'

Well, there are no rules, and if you find it impossible to plan before you begin, and if you can produce satisfactory work without doing so, then there's little point for you in forcing yourself to prepare a synopsis.

But poor construction is a frequent fault among beginners, and my own view is that the majority of them would find it helpful rather than a hindrance to start with a full synopsis. It is a bit like knitting – only the most experienced of knitters would start without a pattern to guide them. They need to be sure the shape, size, colours and tension are right, before they get down to purl and plain and k2 tog. When they start, they know where they are going and for what ultimate purpose.

In fact, I think the difference between the views of those who argue for synopses and of those who are against them is less marked than it might at first appear. I notice that anti-synopsis tutors very often tell their students to ask themselves many of the questions which I regard as an essential part of planning. For instance, in the chapter on the novel in her helpful book *Teach Yourself Creative Writing*, Dianne Doubtfire uses such headings as: *What is the story to be about? Whose story is it?*

What is this person's problem? Where and when does it happen? Where are you going to start? Viewpoint. Plot. The Ending. (Although this list refers to novels, I am sure that Mrs Doubtfire would agree that the same questions could be asked about short stories, or even to some extent about many articles and non-fiction books.) Now, she isn't very keen on working out a plot and is personally dead against a planned ending, saying she seldom knows how her novels will end until she gets there (though I should like to suggest that her subconscious has arrived ahead of her and knows very well!); in other respects, however, she is talking of something very much like the preparation of a synopsis, even if not fully written out.

I, on the other hand, do not begin to write until I know exactly where I am going. Indeed, when I wrote my first novel, *Mario's Vineyard*, I knew the last line of the book before the first, and for all my novels I start with a blow-by-blow summary, several thousand words in length. Only then can I begin the actual writing.

Mrs Doubtfire and I are totally in agreement, however, when she says, 'Choose the way that suits you best.' That is always good advice. And I am certainly not going to say that you will not get published unless your work is planned in advance – many successful authors work as Dianne Doubtfire does. I believe, however, that they are outweighed by those who use a full synopsis, and I remain convinced that careful planning is advisable for beginners, if only because it may save them from false starts and deviations from the story they want to tell.

What about the rigidity of the synopsis? One hears novelists talk of their characters 'taking over', having a life of their own – is it desirable that they should do so, and what happens if they stray badly away from the synopsis? Although I like to know exactly where my story is going and how it will get there, I would never suggest that the synopsis should be so firmly fixed that no changes can be made. It is very exciting when your characters come to life and start behaving in a way you had never expected, or perhaps refusing to do something you had planned. It is one of the great joys of writing and will almost certainly give your work a vitality that it might not otherwise have.

I should point out, firstly, that characters often come to life in this way while I am planning, but if it should happen during the writing stage, I check to see exactly how and where the synopsis must be altered. Sometimes I find that the changes can be accommodated within the original intention, or that the necessary major alteration in the story will strengthen it to a considerable extent. That is fine. On other occasions, I may not be at all happy with the direction in which I am being led, and will go back over the earlier pages to see what I wrote to make the character act in this fashion, which will now have to be changed so that he does not take over the story. Peter Grosvenor, the Literary Editor of the *Daily Express*, tells of asking Iris Murdoch what one does when one's characters start taking over. Ms Murdoch, a firm believer in advance planning replied, 'Well, you must shut them up, dear, shut them up.'

The Chicken or the Egg

No one has been able to find a satisfactory answer to the riddle about the chicken and the egg, but if you are going to write fiction and ask whether the plot or the characters come first, the answer is plain: you must begin with the characters. Obviously, some elements of the story must be there early on – the main theme, the background, the period perhaps – but if you try to devise a detailed plot without first working out the characters, your story will inevitably remain flat and dull. Plot arises out of the characters; it is they and their reactions which cause the narrative to develop.

So begin with the people in your story. This means first of all the central characters – probably few in number. But unless you are writing a short story (and even then in some cases) you will almost certainly need a supporting cast – family, friends, business associates of the protagonists. The main theme of your story will give you a rough idea of how many such people you will need and what sort of part each has to play.

In a later chapter we shall look at characterization and suggest how deeply an author needs to know and understand the characters he creates. At this point, however, let us assume that you have the necessary knowledge and understanding, and concentrate simply on how you are going to manoeuvre them into providing you with a plot.

The essence of drama is conflict, and the same is true of most fiction. One of the most successful basic formulas is to give your central character an ambition of some kind (it may be to marry the hero, or to become rich and successful, or to solve a crime, or to escape from some unpleasant situation), and then place barriers in the way, which have to be overcome before it can be achieved. These obstacles may be caused by external forces (redundancy, for example, or some physical condition such as a flood, or a desert to be crossed), but more often they will arise either from other characters, whose own ambitions may conflict with those of your hero, or from traits in his own character, or both. Since few human beings live without some kind of conflict in their lives, if you build up your characters strongly enough, you will probably find that the barriers arise quite naturally and easily from them.

Another approach is to present the characters that you have created with a crisis, and then see how each would react. 'Oh, I can never imagine anything like that!' But you can, you really can, if you have built up the characters strongly enough in your mind. To give the simplest of examples: if you have devised a very narrow-minded person and then allow something outrageous to happen in front of him, he will react with shock and distaste and perhaps anger. The more you know about him, the easier it will be to imagine what he thinks. And if you can do it for a clearly defined character like that, you can do it for a subtler one too.

Now take it a stage further. The narrow-minded person's reaction will affect other characters in the story. How do they react, not only to the initial crisis, but also to him? Out of actions and reactions you can build your plot. We are all constantly affected by what happens to us and by the people around us, and this means that your characters should develop as the story progresses. Often, in fact, that is the whole basis of the plot – the gradual change that is brought about in the principal character by his experiences.

There is no simple formula for devising a plot – many elements come into it, including sub-plots (which have to be knitted into the main story and must affect it), the time span, the setting, and so on – and the planning of a book can take considerable time and effort, especially as it all has to be controlled and shaped.

Construction

It is sometimes considered old-fashioned nowadays for a piece of writing to have a beginning, a middle and an end. This is largely the result of a vogue for what might be called an open ending, when, instead of tying up all the ends neatly, the author leaves us with questions in our minds. We have all watched those television plays in which, just as things seem to be getting interesting, up come the credits and it is over, leaving us wondering what it was all about (which was probably the playwright's intention). Even those plays, if they are any good, have a beginning, a middle and an end and are carefully constructed.

The next stage in your planning might be to decide where you will begin, where you will end and what will go in between. It will all depend on the story you are going to tell, the facts you want to put across and, most importantly, your characters.

By doing this you will have begun to give *shape* to your work. Jill Paton Walsh, the distinguished writer of children's books, talks of the two parts of an author's mind: the Fabricator, who is the listener and the thrower-up of material; and the Shaper, who constructs an acceptable piece of writing out of the jumble of observations and ideas which the Fabricator supplies. The ability to shape material is an essential part of an author's equipment.

'Shape' is a word which I like very much to apply to writing, precisely because it suggests something which can be seen. I think of it in the form of a line, like that on a graph, which rises and falls as the various points of tension and excitement in your writing come and go. In the case of most fiction, and also in many articles and other non-fiction work, the shape of the line is an ascending one, as you move towards your climax, but if you look at it more closely, you will see a number of peaks and troughs along the way. You may begin with a crisis point of some sort, in which case your line will start high and then perhaps drop down before rising again to the next moment of tension, and down and up, and so on, but climbing each time as you approach the most dramatic part of what you have to say. After that, the line sometimes drops again, as you tie up the ends of the story, or you may prefer to end at the highest point on the graph.

Incidentally, shape exists equally in chapters, paragraphs and sentences, and it is worth trying to see it in them. Chapters very often finish on a rising note of suspense, with the 'cliff-hanger', the device which leaves us wanting to know more; you can hear it each weekday in *The Archers*: when one of the characters says something such as, 'I've just had this letter, and I'm very worried about it, very worried indeed ...', the signature tune follows, and we are left wondering what is in the letter and we tune in the next day to find out. Often, in *The Archers*, the cliff-hanger turns out to be far less interesting than we have been led to believe, which is a pity, even if it has done its job in making us want to hear the next part of the story. The best cliff-hangers lead us on to more excitement and tension.

In sentences and paragraphs, the shape often has an aural quality. Read aloud what you have written, and as your voice rises and falls you may be able to see the shape of the sentence or paragraph in question and judge whether it has the right kind of balance.

Working Out the Shape

Almost anything that is written has a number of high points, whether they are facts to be brought out in non-fiction, or dramatic parts of a novel or short story. But how do you organize them so that they have a shape?

Perhaps the easiest things to decide are the beginning and the end. The story should start just before the sparking point of the main conflict. And the ending is going to be at the climax of the story, or perhaps very shortly after it, when any loose ends have been tied up. But how do you work out what goes in between?

Bearing in mind the main character's aims, ask yourself, 'How can I make this, or that, happen?'. Try to suggest answers: 'What if my character did this?', or 'What if it turned out that ...?' Go on until you find reasonable solutions.

But having settled on the mechanics of your story in this way, you may still need to work out exactly how the various episodes will actually be fitted together into a satisfactory shape. The novelist Winston Clewes once suggested taking a large sheet of paper and setting the numbers 1 to 30 down the left-hand side; write the beginning of your story against 1, and the ending against 30; space the intermediate dramatic points out among the intervening numbers; those numbers which are left (and of course you may not need all of them) are allocated to the linking material between one highlight and the next, the events leading up to and causing each succeeding crisis, and also to the various pieces of background information which you need to put across to the reader. The more exciting you want your story to be, the larger the number of crisis-points, though they will not necessarily all have the same degree of dramatic intensity; some may be the mere revelation of the obstacles which you have placed in the way of your main character's ambition, or their overcoming, while others can be moments of real cliff-hanging excitement.

If you fill in a chart in this way, you will have a kind of synopsis ready-made, and you will also find it easy to translate it into graph form so that you can see the shape you will be working to.

The Tree

Another approach is to think of your work as a tree.

The seed is the first idea, from which the tree will grow.

The trunk is the main theme of what you are writing, and its development.

The top of the tree is the end of the story.

The branches are the characters, the background, the narrative. They are of different sizes, and some of them grow out of each other rather than from the main trunk. And you may not sketch them in ascending order but may take some of the higher ones before lower ones, in rather the same way as Rolf Harris draws little parts of his paintings in an apparently meaningless way, until the whole thing is completed and linked up to make sense.

The metaphor may be a bit strained, but the image of the tree-trunk, straining upwards towards the sky, is perhaps worth remembering – that is the drive, the thrust of whatever you are writing, its core, its *raison d'être*.

Take Your Time

To return to the controversy about whether or not to prepare a synopsis, I think that those tutors who, like Dianne Doubtfire, encourage their pupils simply to go ahead and start writing are right in one way. The most important thing for a beginner is to get used to putting words on paper and to flex that writing muscle. It's very tempting, too, when you are bursting with the beginning of your story or article, or whatever it may be, to sit down and scribble or tap away.

But to do so is probably to jump the gun. Indeed, it may be jumping the gun to rush into the preparation of a synopsis. The origin of most writing is an idea, a spark in the author's brain – often no more than a barely stated theme, or perhaps a vision of some scene in a story – and it needs to be developed. It is worth noting, by the way, that the best writing starts with feelings rather than facts. Anyway, having got your idea, think about it. And don't try to hurry the process. Writing is not just writing – it's thinking too, working things out, discovering the best way to present your ideas, solving some of your problems in advance. All that takes time, especially if you are going to give your subconscious a chance to beaver away, which is nearly always worth doing. As I said in the tree metaphor, the first idea is the seed; well, seeds don't always germinate overnight.

Some authors mull for years over the books they intend to write before putting pen to paper. They believe, as I do, that time spent in planning is never wasted.

4

Making Words Work For You

The Richest Language in the World

Words are wonderful things, with tremendous power to produce reactions, ideas, emotions in the reader. And we who speak and write in English have the special advantage of working with the richest language in the world. We have words of Teutonic origin from the occupation of England by the Angli and Saxons, and Romance-language words from the Norman invasion, and words which have come into use as a result of our past as empire-builders, and we have the influence of our American cousins. Unlike the French, for instance, who make strenuous efforts to keep their language 'pure', we have never been averse to adopting words from any language if they seem useful, with the result that in hundreds of cases English has several words meaning roughly the same thing, but each subtly different in nuance, whereas other languages have far fewer terms, and often only one.

Given this treasure-house of words, one of the great pleasures for the writer of English is, or should be, the selection of those words which will most perfectly express whatever it is that he wants to convey. If Flaubert, with a much more limited language could spend years searching for '*le mot juste*', how much more important it is to choose carefully when you have so many alternatives available.

Let us look at a short passage from *A Distant Trumpet* by Paul Horgan. It describes the people of a small town in Indiana, waiting for a visit by Abraham Lincoln:

'The firehouse band was standing loosely about the station much too early. Now and then a brass horn of the band would squeeze down the sunlight into a single blaze and send it back with a blinding glory.'

How brilliantly selected the word 'loosely' is, and what a fine description of a flash of sunlight on a brass instrument!

Then an extract, every sentence of which has been put together with a careful delight, from Barbara Willard's *The Sprig of Broom*:

It was mid-October, the harvest well stored. The sun was as hot as if it shone in the first week of September, but a tumbling sky threw great clouds before the wind, and when the sun was obscured then all the promise of winter was in the air. But it was magic weather, a gift to sweeten the sadness of the ending year. There were still blackberries, thick and dripping with juice, but these would remain on the bushes, for by now, as it was said, the Devil had spat on them and they should not be eaten. So birds gorged themselves, and the ground and the leaves of the brambles were strewn with purple droppings. The water, half shadow and half glitter, threw back the colours of beech and bracken, tossing them over the boulders like gold and copper coins.'

And look at those well-loved lines from *A Winter's Tale*:

> ... daffodils
> That come before the swallow dares and take
> The winds of March with beauty.

As John Silverlight said in his column in the *Observer*, consider the power and precision of that word 'take'.

Oh, yes, we are lucky to be writing in English! But there are dangers too. In *Reader's Report*, Christopher Derrick wrote, 'By careful choice the writer of English can suggest a fullness and precision of meaning. It is an outstandingly useful language for poetry. *It also offers unparalleled scope for inaccurate and mushy writing* – a splendid language for talking nonsense in, or generating vague verbal fog – the ideal language for a politician.' The italics are mine, inserted so that the reader should not be misled by the slightly jokey tone of the rest of the sentence. Mr Derrick is expressing an important truth.

Probably the best way of avoiding the pitfalls is to examine carefully each word that you use in your writing, making sure that it really does express the meaning you intend and is neither mushy nor inaccurate. It may sound laborious, but it is well worth doing.

Lewis Carroll used words with great care. You will remember that passage in *Through the Looking Glass* when Humpty Dumpty says:

'I mean by "impenetrability" that we've had enough of that subject, and it would be just as well if you'd mention what you mean to do next, as I suppose you don't mean to stop here all the rest of your life.'

'That's a great deal to make one word mean,' Alice said in a thoughtful tone.

'When I make a word do a lot of work like that,' said Humpty Dumpty, 'I always pay it extra.'

He goes on to talk of the words coming round on a Saturday night to get their wages. Nonsense, of course, but Carroll was surely thinking of the care and attention that a writer has to pay to the words he uses, and his ability to make them vary their meaning according to the context and the juxtaposition of other words, and the colour and excitement and inspiration that he can extract from them. Look after the words, pay them well in terms of the trouble you take over them, and they will work willingly and rewardingly for you.

The Spoken and the Written Word

Authors frequently write as they speak, hearing the words in their minds and then putting them down on paper. It generally works very well, but there is one great danger of which you must be aware: in speech you normally have direct contact with your listener, and you provide him with all sorts of signals – intonation and emphasis and facial expressions and sometimes gestures – to help to convey your meaning; you can take a sentence of half a dozen words and say it in a score of different ways, making its meaning totally different each time by the way you use your voice; in conversation there is also the opportunity for the listener to question anything which he does not understand, or on which he would like additional information.

None of this is available to you as a writer – the communication between the author and the reader by means of the written word is indirect, and you therefore have to make sure that your meaning is crystal clear from the words alone.

It is possible to achieve complete clarity and a lack of ambiguity without having to use strings of adverbs and without italics scattered over the page like a rash to indicate the various stresses that you have in mind, but it does mean choosing your words with the utmost care, placing them in exactly the right order, and thereby making it impossible, as far as you can, for the reader to give the words any other interpretation than the one you want.

Interesting Words

I once read a book which suggested at one point that Richard Rodger's success as a composer was partly due to his use of the 'wrong' note. The word 'wrong' was not well-chosen; the author meant that Rodgers made a simple melody more interesting by selecting an *unexpected* note. (The example given was the first bars of 'Oh, What a Beautiful Mornin' ', in which the syllable 'morn' falls on B flat, if the key is C, rather than B natural, which would have been a more normal choice.)

Be that as it may, the use of the unexpected word, the unusual simile or metaphor, can often create a most striking effect.

I remember being taught while at school that one of the tests of a well-written book was to try to guess before you turn the page what the next words will be, the theory being that the better the writer, the more often you will guess wrongly. I am not certain that the case is really proven, but it's an interesting game to play, and it's certainly true that good writers choose their words with the greatest of care, and sometimes startle the reader with the unexpected word or phrase.

As so often, moderation is the watchword. Put in too many unexpected images and you will over-egg the pudding and give your reader mental indigestion. The same applies to the so-called 'four-letter words'. Use them freely, and the result may be a realistic rendering of modern speech patterns, but if your intention is to shock, it won't work. When Shaw wrote the tea-party scene in *Pygmalion*, he gave Eliza only one swear-word to say, not dozens. Words still have the power to shock or to arouse pity or laughter or any number of emotions, but you don't need an army of them – a single word can fight and win a battle on its own, and do so far more effectively than if you had brought all the guns of your vocabulary to bear.

The Weak and the Strong

It may be useful sometimes to think of the relative strengths and weaknesses of the words you use. There are obvious examples in the difference in degrees of meaning between, say, 'fear' and 'terror', or 'misdemeanour' and 'atrocity'. But there are also more subtle strengths and weaknesses. For instance, concrete nouns (the names of objects – 'clock', 'lion', 'village') are usually stronger than abstract nouns (the names of emotions and concepts – 'time', 'neighbourliness', 'pride') precisely because the former conjure up clear pictures before our eyes, whereas abstract nouns concern matters which are more difficult to define and of which we have a much vaguer understanding.

Words which apply to a special kind of person or thing within a group are stronger than the words which apply to the group. As examples, 'whore' is stronger than 'woman', and so in certain contexts is 'lady', and 'oak' is stronger than 'tree'.

Look too at gerunds (those parts of a verb ending in 'ing' which we use as nouns). They have a certain built-in weakness and often lead us into clumsy construction. Take a sentence like 'Be on your guard against his trying to alter your style' – it is not very elegant and would be much stronger if it were changed to 'Be on your guard in case he tries to alter your style.' Gerunds describe something which is in course of happening, a state of being, and that is much weaker than a verb which describes a direct action.

Again, the passive voice of verbs is much less strong than the active voice – 'They were covered with leaves by the birds' is clumsier and provides a less immediate image than 'The birds covered them with leaves'; the second example is direct, the first is indirect. It may be argued that in the second example the emphasis is on 'them', which is where the author intended it should be, rather than on 'the birds'. There may be such valid reasons for selecting the passive, but the active voice is generally to be preferred as being more powerful.

Adjectives and Adverbs

Most beginners use far too many adjectives and adverbs and seem to feel a need to qualify every noun or verb. Of course good and successful writers often make liberal use of adjectives and adverbs; there are plenty of adjectives in that passage from *The Sprig of Broom* quoted earlier in this chapter, and indeed you may see the danger in using too many, because that extract almost goes over the top in its richness – almost, but not quite, because Barbara Willard is a first-class writer and knows what she is doing.

Put in too many adjectives and adverbs and your work risks becoming lush. Re read what you write, see how many adjectives and adverbs you can do without, and make sure that those you leave in are doing a good job for you. ' "Get the hell out of here," she screamed at him angrily.' Do you really need that 'angrily'? And you can increase suspense by the elimination of an adjective or two. Let us suppose that the first line of a story is: 'He would have arrived on time, had it not been for the car accident.' Leave out the word 'car' (which in this example is acting as an adjective), and you immediately increase the suspense by making the reader wonder what sort of accident it was.

The sparer your writing, the more striking it will be. In the story of the Good Samaritan (Luke 10, beginning at verse 30) in the King James Bible there is hardly an adjective in sight, apart from 'certain' and 'other', but how powerful a piece of story-telling it is.

Repetitions

Because our language is so rich, we often find the repetition of words rather clumsy. A glance at a thesaurus can sometimes suggest an alternative word, but you need to make sure that the meaning is not subtly different.

In any case, don't get obsessive about repetitions. Some writers go to such lengths to avoid them that the many alternatives become obtrusive. Repetition is sometimes unavoidable and comparatively harmless. It can also be used deliberately for effect, as in this extract from a Crucifixion scene: 'I watched as they brought him out, that vicious crown of thorns on his brow. I watched as they stripped him and placed him on the cross. I watched as they hammered the nails through the hands and feet.'

Clichés

Some phrases, especially metaphors, are so apposite that, once invented, more and more use is made of them, and eventually they become clichés. 'A hive of industry' provides a marvellous image, based on the proverbial busyness of bees, but it is so much a cliché that we no longer see that image. To put these trite, tired phrases into the dialogue that you write may be acceptable, since natural speech is often full of them, and their use may help you in the creation of a character. Put clichés into the rest of your work, however – 'a cruel twist of fate', 'it suddenly dawned on her', 'as quick as a flash' – and what you write will almost certainly have a flat, uninspired ring to it.

Informality and Slang

Some beginners ask whether it is permissible to use slang in their writing. 'And is it all right to use "can't" and "won't" or must I always say "cannot" and "will not"?'

Of course it's permissible. And of course it's OK.

When you were at school, your teacher may have frowned on the use of slang and informal speech in the compositions you had to write, but you are no longer a schoolchild, there are no rules, and you can please yourself.

You will want your dialogue to sound natural, so you will no doubt include slang and words such as 'shan't' and 'didn't', though if your story has a period setting you must make sure that the slang is not anachronistic, and the fuller form of those negatives – 'shall not', 'did not' and so on – may seem more appropriate for your purposes.

In narrative writing or in journalism, the degree of informality is a matter for your choice but may depend to some extent on the subject and the market for which you are writing. The more serious your approach, the less likely it is that slang will be suitable. But there are no rules. The best arbiter is the ear: read your work aloud or, better still, get someone to read it to you, and listen hard; if the slang and informality sound natural, leave them as they are; if they stick out like sore thumbs, change 'em.

Protecting the Language

Some people feel that we should not accept new words, especially many Americanisms and hideous neologisms such as 'hospitalization'. 'English is rich enough already,' they say, 'and we don't need new words.' But they forget that it is a *living* language, changing and adding to itself all the time. 'Hospitalization', incidentally, may have an ugly sound, but is a very useful word.

At the same time, however willing we may be to accept that our language is alive, writers should do all they can to resist those changes which result in a loss of precision or a weakening of meanings. I have one or two hobby-horses: the difference between 'eager' and 'anxious' – 'I am eager to see you' but 'I am anxious about my health'; 'farther', which implies a greater distance – 'farther along the road' – and 'further', meaning 'additional' – 'a further mile along the road'. The failure to distinguish between 'lie' and 'lay' (and their confusing past versions, 'lay' and 'laid') is very common; the correct usages are: 'I lie on the bed' (present), 'I lay on the bed' (past), 'I lay the parcel down' (present), 'I laid the parcel down' (past). And writers should remember that pictures are 'hung', but men are 'hanged', while in a recent short story competition I would estimate that fifty per cent of the entrants did not know the difference between 'it's', which is the shortened form of 'it is', and 'its', which is the possessive of 'it' – 'The dog had its collar on', not 'it's collar'; 'It's raining', not 'Its raining'. I must also confess that I like to use 'different from' rather than 'different to' or 'different than', despite the fact that the latest editions of *Fowler's Modern English Usage* neatly demolish the case for 'from'.

Spelling and Punctuation

That last paragraph leads directly to the question of spelling and punctuation. Almost all of those who attend classes in Creative Writing freely accept the idea that a writer should love words, but many of them see no necessity to bother very much with spelling and punctuation. I find this hard to understand. A good vocabulary and a feeling for the subtleties of meaning may be the most important tools of the writer's trade, but no one who professes to care for words has the right to neglect punctuation and spelling. It is true that many published authors cannot spell or punctuate, their work being corrected for press by long-suffering editors, but it amazes me that they don't have more pride in their work and want to get it right themselves.

On the other hand, I do recognize that many writers find punctuation and spelling a real bugbear, some being virtually dyslexic. What can you do if you have that problem?

For help with punctuation, read my book, *The Nuts and Bolts of Writing*, which you should find sensible and useful. You may also find it easier to punctuate if you read your work aloud, working on the rough-and-ready basis that where you make a brief pause you will probably need a comma, and for a longer pause a full stop.

The Nuts and Bolts of Writing will again help if your problem is spelling. You should also consult a good dictionary, even when you feel fairly certain that you know how to spell a given word. Incidentally, my agent tells me that the misspelling he notices most frequently in typescripts is 'rythm' instead of 'rhythm'.

If despite reading my *Nuts and Bolts* you still don't know when to use a comma and when a full stop, and if you find constant reference to a dictionary too laborious, ask a friend who *can* spell and punctuate to check your work for you. A teacher would be a good person to ask, especially one who has retired and is ancient enough to have been brought up on old-fashioned lines, with a good grounding in grammar and parsing and parts of speech and all the similar subjects which seem no longer to be taught. If you number such a person among your friends or acquaintances, don't hesitate to ask his help – he will probably be flattered and only too pleased to demonstrate his expertise (though you may have to be on your guard in case he also tries to alter your carefully worked-out style).

Style

What is style, and how do you acquire it?

You already have a natural style. It is simply the way in which you put words together when you are writing, and it may be a direct reflection of your speaking and thinking habits. Some people tend naturally to write in short, staccato sentences, sometimes without using verbs, while others find themselves, without consciously planning to do so, producing a seemingly never ending succession of clauses and sub-clauses before they come to the next full stop, rather in the manner of Henry James, perhaps, or of Bernard Levin.

In *The Way to Write*, John Fairfax and John Moat speak of 'the writer's voice', which is another way of referring to style, and they define it as 'his individual use of language which enables him at last to come at the material which only he can express. It is the hallmark of the accomplished writer and his or her unique authority.' That may strike you as high-flown, but the reference to 'the accomplished writer' bears the implication, correctly, that most writers work on their natural style, refining and polishing it until it is a more subtle and individual instrument than when they first began.

Your style, however perfected and refined it may be, is not immutable, and you may wish to vary it from time to time to suit your subject. Obviously, one writes in short, simple sentences for very young children; not quite so obviously, almost equally short and simple sentences are often used to good effect when exciting action is taking place in an adult novel.

That is all very well, you may say; I can write naturally, or I can vary it according to my subject, but how will I know whether the style is good or not? I can only reply that, if you spend your time worrying about your style, you may never get around to writing at all. Forget about it. Just write. When you have written a first draft, if the writing fits your subject, has a good flow to it and in general seems right at all times, you are probably one of the lucky natural writers and need never bother yourself consciously with style, unless to develop and perfect the gift that you already have.

If, on the other hand, you feel a need to improve your style, what can you do about it? First of all, I think you need to feel sure that the shape of what you write and its rhythms are satisfactory.

When, in the chapter on Planning, I discussed 'shape', I was referring to the overall picture, the rise and fall of tension throughout the work. Although I am now thinking in the much smaller terms of phrases, sentences and paragraphs, the same kind of principles apply. Make sure that the shape of the sentence is right, that the emphases come in the right place, that you have not wandered to such an extent that the end of the sentence no longer seems to relate to its beginning. And check the relationship between the sentences to see that the narrative flow is maintained.

You can look at the shape of a sentence in a different way: it may have a very simple construction, consisting simply of a subject, a verb and an object ('I love you', for example), or it may be very complex with all kinds of sub-clauses and other trimmings ('I, the son, and the fourth son at that, of an impoverished woodcutter, and having therefore no fortune to boast of, despite my lowly birth and the fact that my fairy godmother expressly forbade me to make such a declaration to anyone of higher standing than a shepherdess, wish to state that I love you will all my heart ...' etc, for a bad example).

Again, the shape should be something that you can see in terms of a line on a graph, but you have an additional advantage in this case in that you can see the physical pattern of the words you have written on the page, and can look at them to see how the sentences and paragraphs balance against each other. Sight always seems to me to be helpful to a writer in this limited sense of looking at the physical shape of what you write. Hearing is even more valuable. Read your work aloud; you can sometimes *hear* the shape, and you should certainly be able to make out its rhythms. You need to have variety, and please be particularly on the watch for the common fault of a number of consecutive sentences of exactly the same length and shape and rhythm.

Simplicity and Brevity

On the whole, the more simply and briefly you try to write, the more effective your writing is likely to be. Churchill once said that no sentence should be more than nine words long. I cannot believe that he really meant it, unless perhaps he was thinking of journalism for one of the down-market papers or was trying to stifle the prolixity of his ministers or their civil servant advisers.

To keep sentences down to a mere nine words may be going too far. At the same time, if in doubt, always err on the side of brevity, and if your natural style entices you toward the long, convoluted sentence, be sure that you retain clarity in your writing.

Simplicity often means using the Anglo-Saxon word rather than the one derived from Latin, but, as with almost everything in this chapter, and indeed throughout the whole book, no hard and fast rule can be made. Sometimes the longer, more formal-sounding word of Romance derivation is needed for the sake of precision or for variety or because of some special effect that it creates. Nevertheless, if you look at any piece of gobbledegook – one of those incomprehensible sets of instructions, or sub-section something-or-other of such-and-such an Act – you will usually find that half the problem is that the language used seems to contain every long, Latin-derived word that the author could dredge up.

The Writers' Duty Towards the Language

The history of words, their derivations, the way they change meanings – these things should be of vital interest to any writer. He should love dictionaries and thesauruses and books like *Brewer's Dictionary of Phrase and Fable*, and he should enjoy word-games and perhaps crossword-puzzles (though please don't worry if you can't abide them). He should be fascinated by the things that other writers do with words – especially those authors whose greatness is widely acknowledged. (Incidentally, it is an interesting fact that an over-familiar or even apparently 'dull' classic may suddenly become newly alive for you if you start to analyse the way its author used words.) He should also be interested in the sound of words, and should be aware, especially when reading his own work aloud, of the aural effect which individual words and phrasings can have.

More than all that, the writer should take pleasure in working with words himself, playing with them, seeing what he can achieve with them. In short, making them work for him.

And he should always remember that we are all custodians of our language, and we exercise our custodianship every time we speak, but far more importantly and influentially when we write. It is a responsibility which should be taken seriously.

5

How Many Words?

The Daily Count

When I first started on my career as an author, I read John Braine's book *Writing a Novel*. It contains a great deal of common sense about writing, and I found it very useful, but it gave one piece of advice – no, an *instruction* – which I thought was absolute nonsense. John Braine insisted that a writer should count the number of words he wrote each day. I couldn't see how that would help in any way.

However, I have found this 'nonsense' to be of immense value, and for several reasons. Firstly, a writer should, I believe, be aware of what kind of output he can achieve – the more you know about the way you write, the more control over it you have. Secondly, the length of what you write may be a crucial factor in your ability to sell it, and by counting the words you write each day, you may get some idea of whether you are going to meet the target length. Thirdly, as John Braine points out, counting words is a spur – 'What prevents most first novels from being written,' he says, 'is the sheer magnitude of the task, the writer's feelings that such a huge achievement isn't within the realm of possibility. The record of a steadily growing number of words dispels this feeling.' He then goes on to say that a writer should set himself a daily target and suggests a minimum of 350 words. Personally, I prefer a weekly target, but I still count my output each day. It is on the following day that I find it so stimulating: if I have previously had a bad day and written very little or even nothing at all, then I determine to do better than that; if I have had an average or a good day, then I tell myself that I must at least maintain that rate of progress. Incidentally, I never relax once I have reached my weekly target – it is a minimum, not a stopping-point.

When you finish for the day, you may find it helpful to stop while you are still in full flow – even in mid-sentence – the idea being that it is then easier to start again the next day. Even if you have trained yourself into the habit of writing, there are mornings when it seems more necessary to sharpen your pencils, or file your letters, or simply look out of your window at the world outside. Such distractions are far less tempting if you stopped the previous day knowing what comes next and eager to get on with it.

How Long?

There is a story that a new author telephoned a publisher to ask: 'How long is an average novel?' 'About seventy-five thousand words,' the publisher replied. 'Thank God,' said the writer, 'I've finished!'

When I am asked, as I frequently am, how long a novel should be, I always reply that it should be as long as it wants to be. Not as long as you, the author, think it should be; not necessarily as long as the publisher wants it to be; but as long as the novel itself wants to be, consisting of as many words as are needed to tell the story without any feeling that you have either skimped, in order to keep the wordage down, or padded, in order to bump it up. Please note, by the way, that I am talking about final drafts – earlier versions may well not be the length that the book really wants to be, and, since most authors tend to overwrite at first, may shrink considerably once you start your revision (see Chapter 6). This suggestion that the book itself knows best about its ideal length, I continue, applies to any kind of writing -- articles, short stories, non-fiction books of all kinds – and not just novels.

There is a lot to be said for that answer, but it is perhaps a little slick. It doesn't always apply. If you write romantic fiction for Mills & Boon, for instance, you will have to restrict your novel to 50–55,000 words. If your book is to be published as part of a series, you may well have to write to a fixed length (and, indeed, to a formula as far as the contents of the book are concerned). And if you are writing articles or short stories for the magazine market, you will almost certainly need to work out in advance what kind of length is likely to be acceptable.

Nevertheless, even if you are restricted for some reason to a specific length, the space needed for what you want to say should still be paramount. If you are aiming at 50,000 words but your story has come out at, say, 40,000, it would take an awful lot of padding to increase it by twenty-five per cent, and it would probably be very obvious that it had been padded; instead, you may have to invent some new dimension to the story, going back to the beginning if necessary and replanning and rewriting. Equally, if your work is very much overlength, although cutting may be both possible and beneficial, it won't be easy if you have already written tightly, and you may be forced into a more radical solution, such as cutting out some element in your plot.

Of course, length is partly dictated by subject. If you aim to write a 60,000 word novel (probably the minimum acceptable length, apart from romances), don't try to cram into it a plot which involves dozens of characters, each with problems to be worked out, and many different backgrounds and time changes. Equally, for a really long book, you will need more than a very simple story. That may seem to be stating the obvious, but both these problems do occur, and many first novels do not get finished either because as John Braine said, their authors are overwhelmed by the magnitude of the task, or because they run out of story before they run out of steam.

Chapters

There *must* be at least twenty chapters in a novel, Mr Braine says, and 'each must end with a hook to draw you on into the next chapter.' I would more or less agree with the second proposition, but the first really is nonsense, and no publisher would reject a book simply because it had fewer than twenty chapters. There are no rules of this kind. Most publishers of light fiction like a reasonable number of chapters, because the breaks make for easier reading, but many successful books have been published without any chapters at all. Or look at Nicholas Monsarrat's last completed novel, the first volume of *The Master Mariner* – it consists of well over 200,000 words but is divided into a mere seven chapters. You may think that Monsarrat got away with that because he was so well established and that a beginner would be frowned upon if he produced similar 30,000-word chapters. But Monsarrat's experience and popularity had nothing to do with it. He 'got away with it' because the material in each chapter belonged together, was a single entity and could not reasonably have been divided; and each chapter ended at a point when all that material had been presented to the reader, leaving nothing further to be said.

So how long should a chapter be? As long as it wants to be. In other words, as long as it needs to be in order to present all the material in that section of your book which belongs together and is a single entity. It may be very long, or it may be very short, and there is no rule either to say that all the chapters in a book must be even roughly of the same length. A chapter may be based on one particular character or group of characters, or on a certain event or set of events, or on a period in time, or it may be related to the moments of crisis in the story. And its length is not determined in any arbitrary way but by the fact that after a while you come to what television has taught us to call 'a natural break'.

The natural breaks in popular TV programmes come at points in the stories which, if you think about it, are like the ends of chapters in a book. Look for the natural breaks in your own writing, and you will almost certainly have found your chapter ends, especially if they coincide with a cliff-hanger, or the hook of which John Braine speaks.

Paragraphs and Sentences

A paragraph usually (but not always – once again there are no firm rules) embodies one thought and its immediate development, and it should end when you have said all you have to say about one thought and are ready to embark on a new one.

But bear in mind that paragraphing is sometimes done for cosmetic reasons. Too large a chunk of solid text can be very off-putting to the reader, so a very long paragraph is sometimes split rather arbitrarily into shorter pieces. In the more popular newspapers paragraphs are rarely longer than two or three short sentences.

The paragraphing of dialogue does have some rules – or at least, near-rules – and these will be covered in the chapter on dialogue.

Just as to begin a new chapter should be to re-awaken the reader's interest, a new paragraph gives emphasis to what it says. Again it may be helpful to think of this in aural terms. Read any piece of prose aloud and there should be a distinct change of tone with each new paragraph. Better still, listen to the news on radio; each news item forms a paragraph, and the slight pause between them alerts us to the change of subject and gives importance to the next headline.

Note the relative strengths and weaknesses of the sentences within a paragraph, or the phrases within a sentence. Generally speaking, the last sentence in a paragraph, or phrase in a sentence, is more emphatic than the first, which in turn is weightier than those in between.

Traditionalist grammarians used to insist that sentences should not begin with 'and' or 'but'; it was even more of a sin to begin a paragraph with a conjunction. Like many other grammatical shibboleths, this one is often ignored nowadays, but you should be aware that, when you begin a sentence, or particularly a paragraph, with 'and' or 'but' you are giving a slightly different emphasis to what follows; you are saying that, though the material is connected to what came immediately before, it is not so closely connected that it has to be visually linked. And this again puts a little more stress on your new sentence or paragraph.

6

Revision

The Hardest Lesson

When people first begin to write, they usually want to get everything down on paper as fast as possible. Later they realize that there is much to be gained by thinking about it first, and maybe planning the work in some detail. But the most difficult concept for the beginner to accept seems to be the idea of *rewriting* – and rewriting not once, not twice, but as many times as necessary to get the work as near perfection as you can manage.

At many Writers' Circles, aspiring authors read out their work and listen attentively to the comments they receive. You can learn a great deal from what is said about your work and about other people's, even if the criticism is sometimes confusing, different advice coming from everyone who speaks. But that is usually as far as it goes. The author takes his piece of writing home, files it or tears it up and starts thinking about a new effort to be written in time for the next meeting. He would learn even more, and make better progress, if he tried, having decided which of the comments made were really valid, to rewrite his piece in a serious effort to improve it. And he should do that before going on to write anything else.

Revision is hard work – there's no getting away from it. The first draft – when you let everything pour out onto the page, following your plan but still allowing yourself freedom to vary it as you go along, and not worrying about all the rough edges – this is the most exciting part of writing, and the most creative. But you can't have fun all the time. Anything that is worth doing is worth doing well, and nothing that is worth doing well can be done without effort.

How to Revise

The first thing to do is – nothing. Put your work away for as long as you can bear – preferably for about three months. This may not be possible, because of a deadline, but try to have a gap, however short, between completing the first draft and beginning the revision. Then, when you come back to the piece, it will be less familiar to you than when you had just finished writing it, and you have a better chance of seeing it with the eyes of a stranger, or indeed of your ultimate reader. As Marcus Quintillian said nearly two thousand years ago, 'There can be no doubt that the best method of writing is to lay our literary compositions aside for a while, that we may after a reasonable period return to them, and find them, as it were, altogether new to us.' Returning to your work after a lapse of time, you will probably see all sorts of things wrong in it that had not occurred to you before.

Another advantage in this delay is that it gives your subconscious time to work. Get on with something else, if you can, forget about what you have just finished, and let it lie fallow. Some of the things that happen beneath the surface of your brain in this period can be absolute magic. Although you are not consciously working on it, all kinds of ideas for its improvement may suddenly come to you.

When you do come to revise, you must be as self-critical and ruthless as you possibly can, and you should devote all possible time and care to the job. Read a passage through to look for general faults, and then break it down into smaller units, and even into the single words, examining every part to see that it is doing a really faultless job for you.

I have always found it most helpful to read my work aloud, because the ear hears such things as infelicitous phrasing and awkward rhythms and repetitions which the eye may not see. If my first draft were not such a mess, I would get someone else to read it to me. The advantage of doing this is that someone reading your work for the first time may not immediately recognize the expression and the emphases which you could hear in your mind as you wrote the words. If the work doesn't sound the way you intended, you will need to rewrite.

What Do You Need to Alter?

You might begin by making a list of the qualities one looks for in good writing, and then checking to see how well your work measures up. A brief list might include the following:

Clarity. The ability to convey thoughts, ideas, stories to others without ambiguity.

Simplicity. This is largely a matter of syntax and grammar and style (see Chapter 4).

Construction. A beginning, a middle and an end, or at least a feeling that the work progresses logically through to the end, and that there is some sense of fulfilment in that ending.

Rhythm. Variety in the pace of the book, in the choice of words and the way they have been put together, and the construction of chapters or particular incidents in the overall story.

Interest and Colour. The quality of the content, or the style or both. The dramatic presentation of the narrative which makes us want to go on reading.

Examining your work under these headings, you will perhaps see, if you are ruthlessly honest with yourself, that it does not measure up as well as you had hoped. Since the qualities in the list apply broadly to the whole work, it may seem that you are going to be involved in rewriting the whole thing, or at least a substantial part of it. But before you do so, take comfort from the fact that major failings can sometimes be cured by attention to apparently minor faults. And the first place to start is by asking yourself whether you have been guilty of over-writing. Don't despair – we nearly all do it, and it can be put right. Take out your blue pencil.

Cutting

Cut anything which can come out without in any way damaging the impact of what you have written or the main points which you need to get across to the reader. You may be able to dispense with huge chunks of unnecessary verbiage, and although it may be difficult to be ruthless when it has taken you so much time and effort to get the words down on paper, the result will almost certainly be a vast improvement. Indeed, it is astonishing to see how much more life and colour and excitement you can get into most pieces of writing by cutting as little as five per cent – an average of $1\frac{1}{2}$ lines on a normal A4 double-spaced page. As Sydney Smith said, 'In composing, as a general rule, run your pen through every other word you have written; you have no idea what vigour it will give to your style.'

Cut all those unnecessary adjectives and adverbs. See page 43.

Cut all the sentences which explain to the reader something which should be self-evident. I have a tendency in the early drafts of my novels to give a character a line of dialogue and then to follow it by explaining what was in his mind as he said it. Sometimes of course, this can be effective, when his thoughts and his speech differ in some way, but very often I am simply explaining something which the reader can work out for himself (and enjoys working out for himself – don't ever underestimate the pleasure that a reader gets from the understanding which he contributes when he is reading).

Cut your research when it shows. Never give more background details than are necessary for the reader's comprehension of the situation. (See page 96.)

Cut anything which does not have a strict relevance to what you are writing. Every word should be there for a purpose.

Cut what I call 'habit' words and phrases, such as 'in fact' and 'of course' and 'obviously', which are often unnecessary. (Yes, I know there are too many of them in this book.)

Cut the things you like best. According to Samuel Johnson, an old tutor of a college said to one of his pupils, 'Read over your compositions, and wherever you meet with a passage which you think is particularly fine, strike it out,' and Arthur Quiller-Couch said, 'Murder your darlings.' It may sound absurd at first, not to mention harsh, but it's excellent advice, because it's really telling you not to be self-indulgent.

Cut the first and last paragraphs of anything you have

written, and see whether you really notice their absence. You may need to put them straight back again (especially the first paragraph if you have used it, as you should, to intrigue and 'hook' your reader), but your piece may work more effectively without them. This advice applies particularly to your final paragraphs, for many writers feel it necessary to end the story by telling the reader things that he can work out for himself quite satisfactorily. If you are writing a fairy story, you may have to follow the convention and add that 'they were married and lived happily ever after', but for most adults the interest is over when the slipper fits Cinderella's foot.

Other Revision

Repetitions. This is not just a matter of words or phrases which jar because they are repeated within a very short distance of each other, but also of making sure that you have not unintentionally told the reader the same thing twice.

Consistency. The most experienced of authors can, for instance, start by giving his heroine eyes of blue and later change them to green, or can alter a character's age or habits. Timing and seasons bring many problems (don't make daffodils bloom in summer or forget that the passage of time brings physical change), and you need to remember where people and objects are at any given moment. I once wrote a story in which the hero cycled to a friend's house, went out in the friend's car and was eventually driven back to his own cottage. The next morning, he got on his bike and rode off to somewhere else. My wife pointed out that the bike was still at the friend's house.

I also include under this heading the need to be consistent in spelling and the use of capital letters and the way you set out headings and sub-headings. I find it useful, when writing something in which certain words appear quite often, to make a list of them so that I use the same form each time. For instance, for this book I made myself a note to use 'rewriting' rather than 're-writing' and 'Creative Writing' rather than 'creative writing'.

Awkward Phrasing and Ambiguities. Elimination of these will help to achieve both clarity and simplicity. Look especially for the long and involved sentence where one is not sure which noun an adjectival clause or phrase should be attached to, or the kind of sentence in which the pronoun 'he' could refer to any one of three males in the story.

Overlong Passages. Sometimes a paragraph seems to go on for ever but may contain no single word which can be cut. It may be a long speech in dialogue, which would work better if interrupted by a small piece of descriptive material – a sentence such as 'He walked to the window' may serve to break up what would otherwise sound like an endless monologue. Or a descriptive passage may need to be divided by a line of dialogue to avoid a monotonous effect. Inordinately long paragraphs are unattractive to the reader, which is another reason for splitting them up, but don't fall into the opposite error of making all your paragraphs very short. Keep a balance.

Underwriting. Although the tendency of most authors is to overwrite, there are nearly always occasions when you will find passages in your first draft which need further expansion. This can happen, especially if you have worked out your story in detail before you begin, because you know everything about it and have written it with that background knowledge, forgetting that your reader may need some things explained which you have taken for granted. Or you may simply have missed an opportunity, as in one of my novels when I described a death in a few lines – 'You must make more of this,' my editor told me. 'Spin it out, wallow in it, show us the pathos, let us see your hero overcome by grief at the passing of this man. Your reader should be weeping buckets when he finishes the chapter.' My editor was right, and I tried again. Of course, I have to admit that if, while writing the book, I had remembered constantly that excellent advice to 'make a scene of it', my editor would not have had to point out a missed opportunity.

Tidying up. After you have cut here and added there and rewritten this bit and twisted this back to front, you need to go through carefully, making sure that everything still works. Some passages may need to be re-linked, or sometimes a name substituted for a pronoun, and so on.

Revising as You Write

I have so far talked of revision as though it can be done only once the first draft is on paper. Some authors like to do the donkey work as they go along. Nicholas Monsarrat used to write precisely six hundred words a day; he got up early, worked all the morning, and by lunch-time six hundred words were not merely on paper but so polished that he never changed them again afterwards. Mind you, he had the whole of the novel most carefully planned in note form and in his head, so he did not have the problem of finding that he had written a passage which was unnecessary or out of balance with the rest of the work, or that one of the characters had taken over and was altering the course of the story – all the details had been worked out and controlled in his mind before he started writing.

Of course, there is no reason at all why you should not revise as you go along, and many writers do it to some degree, which is why first drafts are so often almost incomprehensible, because of all the crossings-out and additions and alterations. But for the majority this revision-as-you-go-along technique does not eliminate the need for a thorough rewrite later.

And – let me say it again – I am not talking of just one rewrite but of many. One is hardly ever enough. The better you can make your work, the better its chances of publication, and that means just as many revisions as you have time for, or until you feel you can do no more.

But if you think that, I should be surprised. I have met no good writer who is ever satisfied with what he has written.

7

The Novel – General Principles

How Do I Tell My Story?

One of the best pieces of advice I know on how to tell a story was given by the publisher Michael Joseph. In her autobiography, Monica Dickens tells how Mr Joseph signed her up to write her first book, which was to be an account of her experiences as a daily 'help'. She told him she did not know how she was actually going to put on paper what she wanted to write. 'Don't be afraid,' he said. 'Imagine a roomful of people you know quite well and saying, "Do you *know* what happened to me?" "No, what?" "It was like this." And you tell it. Don't worry about *how* to write. Just write.'

Of course, Monica Dickens already knew what she was going to say, and her story, since it was about a particular set of experiences, was already complete in all its essentials. She was not worrying about what her story was, but how to put it into words. If, however, you are trying to write something original, something which you are inventing, then, as I have already said, it is worth spending some time before you begin in working out exactly what you are going to say. Then take Michael Joseph's advice.

The Focus of Attention

One of the first things you will have to decide is from what point of view you will tell your story. You have four choices: you can use a character telling the story in the first person; you can tell the story in the third person but seeing its events through the eyes of your main character; again in the third person, you can take what has become known as 'the God's eye view', when, instead of seeing the story through a single character's eyes, you tell it through your own eyes as author, seeing all, understanding all, explaining all; the fourth choice is a combination of two or more of the other three.

The first-person technique has great advantages and great drawbacks. It gives a great sense of immediacy, and many writers, especially beginners, find it easier to project themselves completely into their main character if they can write their story, as it were, in his or her name (to have a first-person narrator, incidentally, rarely works well if he or she is not the main character and is merely a spectator of the other characters' actions); on the other hand, if you write in the first person, you can put into your story only things which are experienced by or personally known to that character, which can be very limiting.

The God's eye view gives the author great freedom but is inclined to be remote and dispassionate. To take just one example, this is the technique which tends always to describe scenery or emotions impersonally rather than through the eyes of the main character. The main failing of the God's eye view, however, is that it often leaves the reader in some confusion as to which characters he is supposed to be interested in, which is a matter of considerable importance (see pages 71-2). And much the same applies if you use a combination of methods.

The most frequently used (and generally most successful) technique is the narrative in the third person with a concentration on the viewpoint of a single character, on whom your attention, and that of the reader, is focused. It is possible in a novel to switch the viewpoint from one character to another, but in general when you do this you should stay with the new character for the whole of the chapter or at least the scene concerned. To switch the point of view in the middle of an episode is very confusing.

Action or Narration?

The novelist has a great deal in common with the dramatist. He should be interested in conflict and suspense, and when those elements are apparent in his story, he should present them to the reader before his very eyes, as it were, just as a dramatist puts the main dramatic events of his play on the stage rather than letting them happen off-stage and then having to tell the audience that they have taken place.

So action (when the event is described as it actually takes place) is infinitely preferable to narration (when the author reports the event indirectly). But you won't be able to turn everything in your story into action. If you have used Winston Clewes' thirty-point technique, as described in the chapter on Planning, the parts of your story which you noted down first, the high points, will almost certainly be scenes, while the linking material in between may be best done as narration. To some extent you need to experiment – after dramatizing the whole of one of your big moments of tension, you may discover that the first part of it would be better in narrative form, simply because it is very difficult to keep excitement at boiling-point for a long time and because the excitement when you do get to it in its dramatic form may be all the more tense in contrast to the flatter narrative which precedes it.

Let us take an example. Suppose in your novel you have a trial scene (always good for conflict and drama). You may be tempted to present everything that happens in court in dramatic form, right from the beginning, but in fact much of that may be very dull, and the interest will come only, for instance, when one of your principal characters appears in the witness box. It is probably better to write something such as:

'The trial droned on through the first morning. Mr Bird, the solicitor for the prosecution, seemed ill at ease, stumbling his way lengthily through the case against Philip and then calling the police sergeant to the witness box almost as though surprised to find his name among his papers. The sergeant's evidence was brisk and efficient, his manner contrasting sharply with Mr Bird's bumbling approach. John Preston remained seated – nothing that the sergeant had said could possibly be challenged – but he gave Philip a little smile and nod of reassurance. The next witness was Jennifer.'

That, perhaps, is where the drama and the fun begin, and you will give us a blow-by-blow description of it, using a great deal of dialogue to make a dramatic scene of it.

Better still, by the way, in that example, would be something like this:

'The trial droned on through the first morning. Mark thought that Mr Bird, the solicitor for the prosecution, seemed ill at ease, stumbling his way lengthily through the case against Philip and then calling the police sergeant to the witness box almost as though surprised to find his name among his papers. The sergeant's evidence was brisk and efficient, his manner contrasting sharply with Mr Bird's bumbling approach. When he had told his story, Mark looked anxiously at John Preston. Surely he would challenge the evidence? But the barrister remained seated, though he gave Mark a little smile and nod of reassurance. The next witness was Jennifer. Mark sat up.'

The difference in the second version is, of course, that the scene is now narrated through Mark's eyes – the focus of attention is on him. It is always better to let your story develop through your characters and their actions, rather than narrating it yourself in your capacity as author.

In fact, wherever possible, the author needs to keep out of it. Part of your object in writing fiction may be to put across some point of view, but it won't work if you do it as the author. You will have to let one of your characters make your points for you, and that means creating the kind of person who would hold whatever opinions he is going to present. Don't lecture the reader, either, or give any indication of your own expertise in a given subject – let it all come out through your characters. And do note that, except in dialogue, the use of an exclamation mark is often an intrusion by the author, who is saying to the reader, 'Isn't this exciting/funny/sad/or whatever?' Let the reader work it out for himself.

Suspense

Suspense exists in all good fiction, and not just in the thrillers which are sometimes called 'suspense stories'. It is quite simply the desire that a successful author creates in the reader to know what happens next.

The most obvious form of suspense, already mentioned, is the 'cliff-hanger' where a character is left at the end of a chapter or section in the middle of a tense situation of some kind. After all, the term came from serial films, where the heroine would be left clinging precariously to a cliff-face at the end of a reel, and one would have to wait until next week to discover how she escaped.

But, useful though this device is, a more continuous way of keeping the reader's interest must be found, and this can perhaps be best done by working out a plot which contains a large amount of continuous conflict and which, at least for a large part of the story, is unpredictable as far as the reader is concerned.

Conflict between the hero or heroine and his or her aims, or between one character and another (especially effective if they are related or close friends), creates tension and interest, and the more sympathetic your hero or heroine and the greater the problems that they have to face, the more strongly will the suspense factor operate.

As for unpredictability, this works particularly well if you can lead the reader to believe that something is inevitably about to happen, and then provide a surprise which takes your characters into a situation other than the one he had expected.

You do have to be careful, however, that the conflict and the twists and turns of the plot are not arbitrary, by which I mean that they should arise out of the characters in the story and their reactions to each other and to outside events. You must also beware of introducing too many surprises, which will cause the reader to stop believing in the story and its characters.

Most readers of fiction are prepared to grant the author a suspension of disbelief, meaning a willingness to accept something which would normally be incredible, or at least strange enough to raise a sceptical eyebrow. But there are always limits to what can be swallowed in this way. Moreover, if you ask a reader to suspend his disbelief over some fact which is central to your story, you must keep within the conventions that you have established.

To clarify that, let me cite the example of a horror story on which I collaborated with another author. The main idea was a variation on the Faust theme – a group of people who had made a pact with the Devil, exchanging their souls for immortal life. Readers of that kind of story are usually perfectly willing to suspend disbelief and accept such a pact as being real. But everything else in the novel had to be written within the convention – the characters had to believe in the pact and their immortality and the looming presence of the Devil, who would eventually demand retribution from them, and they had to behave accordingly. The problems came when we introduced outsiders (our hero and heroine) into the community, because the place and the people there had to appear normal to them, and that meant a conflict with the convention we had established.

Suspense can effectively be introduced by not revealing at the beginning all the information that the reader needs, and this is one of the most useful devices in the writer's technique. Sure that there must be more to learn, the reader's interest is aroused and he wants to read on. Charles Reade gave excellent advice when he said, 'Make 'em laugh. Make 'em cry. But make 'em *wait.*'

Suppose you start a story with the words, 'When I think of Miriam, the first thing I remember is her startling appearance.' The reader immediately has a number of questions in his mind: who is the 'I' of this story? what sort of person is Miriam? and, above all, what was startling about her appearance? Or suppose the first sentence is even simpler – 'I often wonder what happened to Miriam.' The same kind of questions are raised, and the reader's interest is bolstered by his belief that an author wouldn't begin like that if the subsequent story were not worth the telling.

Another reason, of course, for not telling the reader everything at the beginning is that, if you give him too much detail early on, it may prove indigestible and easily forgotten, whereas information released in small doses gives him the pleasurable feeling that he is making discoveries.

Sometimes information is deliberately held back by the author because he feels it will be better to give it in the form of a flashback. Flashbacks can be very effective, and their use is quite legitimate if it increases suspense. Otherwise, they are probably best avoided, simply because they complicate the narrative unnecessarily.

Suspense is also created by dramatic irony. This is the term used when an audience, or the reader, is aware of something which the characters in the story do not yet know. For instance, if the reader knows that the villain is waiting round the next corner with a meat-axe, he will read with more than usual interest a description of the hero strolling along without a care in the world, blissfully unaware of what is waiting for him. He will want to know what happens next. The dramatic irony has created suspense.

Little Clouds

In the most satisfying kind of detective story, clues to the identity of the murderer are gradually woven into the story. They must not be too obvious, but part of the pleasure lies in picking them up, so that at the end you can say, 'I thought so,' and congratulate yourself on your astute observation. The same technique is used in most kinds of writing. A hint is dropped early on to prepare the reader for what is to come later. As Chekhov said, 'If you're going to fire a gun in the third act, your audience must see it loaded in the first.' But it need not be as dramatic-sounding as that. In one of my novels I intended that a character would emerge at a fairly late stage in the story as a designer of fabrics; soon after she first appeared in the novel, I dropped in the information that she was fond of drawing and painting, and later there was another brief reference to her artistic talent; the point was not laboured on either occasion, and indeed the reader may have wondered why the matter had been mentioned at all (a minor example of the creation of suspense, though that was not the object of the exercise), but when the time came for the character to start the design work, the reader was ready, I hope, to accept it as natural that someone with her talents and interests would be likely to undertake it.

It was Charles Morgan, I believe, who first spoke of this technique in terms of 'a little cloud like a man's hand'. He was referring to the story in Chapter 18 of the First Book of Kings:

> And Elijah said unto Ahab, Get thee up, eat and drink; for there is a sound of abundance of rain. So Ahab went up to eat and to drink. And Elijah went up to the top of Carmel; and he cast himself down upon the earth, and put his face between his knees, and said to his servant, Go up now, look toward the sea. And he went up, and looked, and said, There is nothing. And he said, Go again seven times. And it came to pass at the seventh time, that he said, Behold there ariseth a little cloud out of the sea, like a man's hand. And he said, Go up, say unto Ahab, Prepare thy chariot, and get thee down, that the rain stop thee not. And it came to pass in the mean while, that the heaven was black with clouds and wind, and there was a great rain.

'Little clouds' can be of tremendous value, and readers are astonishingly good at recognizing such clues and storing them away in their minds for later reference. The element of surprise is not necessarily destroyed, because it is no more than a hint, a *little* cloud, not a thundering great sky-filling cumulo-nimbus. It justifies the surprise, when it comes, but it doesn't anticipate it.

The reader's readiness to pick up little clouds also means that there is a danger in dropping in pieces of information which do not later turn out to have any significance. The reader is then likely to feel that he has been conned into taking notice of something unimportant. I was presented once in a Creative Writing class with a story, quite well written, which began with two girls waiting on a railway platform; a high wind tore away the scarf that one of them was wearing and carried it out of her reach; then the train came in and the story progressed, but there was no further mention of the scarf. I pointed this out and asked why the author had put the episode in. 'Just to show how strong the wind was,' she replied. 'Then in fact you have provided us with two unfulfilled little clouds,' I told her. 'One is the wind, because you don't use the fact that it is strong in any other way in the story; and the other – quite a big cloud in fact, since you place a lot of emphasis on it – is the scarf blowing away.' The lesson is that nothing irrelevant should go into your writing.

Little clouds can often be introduced into dialogue with great effect, when characters give some hint of their interests or traits which you will use later in your story.

Don't Put Everything In

I have already emphasized that little clouds should indeed be little. Never underestimate the reader's intelligence and his ability to work things out for himself. Leave things unsaid. Let the reader read between the lines. If you use some telling contrast – a scene of Nazi leaders living in luxury, followed by a passage set in a concentration camp, for example, or an extremely unhappy person finding himself caught up in other people's gaiety – you don't have to point out the irony. The reader will see it for himself. Never, never *explain*. If you have to explain *what* you have written, it means that you haven't written it clearly in the first place. If you try to explain *why* you wrote it, you are insulting the reader's intelligence.

Remember too that you are not providing a photographic story of real life. Fiction focuses on certain aspects of the story it tells and the characters in that story. The author's job is not to put in every tiny detail, to report all the minutiae of life, but to select, and he must ensure that everything he chooses to put into his writing is there for a purpose.

Don't put anything in a novel, or indeed any kind of writing, which hasn't a good reason for being there; that includes not putting any sort of emphasis on characters who are little more than 'extras' (in the sense that the word is used in the cinema). People are always interesting, and if you introduce and describe and name them, they act like little clouds and distract from the other characters and incidents in the story that we should be interested in. Sometimes you will need very minor characters, but you can signal to the reader that they are unimportant and that he need not concern himself with them by not naming them or giving any detailed descriptions.

Where to Begin

It is vital to grab the reader's attention from the very beginning, and this is why you should start your story just before a moment of crisis. Better still, start at the moment of crisis itself, plunging the reader straight into the story at a point of tension when he will immediately want to know what happens next. If you try to set the scene, or give us the history of what led up to the crisis, or even if you introduce us to the characters in any detail, you risk not getting your hooks into the reader firmly enough. And once you've got them in, you must keep them there. Keep the tension in the scene going. Of course you will have to get all the background information across sooner or later, but let it come out gradually, rather than in a great indigestible lump. Much of it may not need to be told at all in the first chapter.

Introduce your principal character as soon as possible. The sooner the reader knows which person he is supposed to be interested in, the better. And beware of bringing in too many characters too early. I once read an opening chapter of a novel in which, although it was not overlong, the author presented the reader with no fewer than twenty-seven named characters, and since he gave each of them roughly the same amount of description and prominence, there was no way of knowing which were important and which minor. He revised the chapter successfully, cutting a number of characters who were not necessary to his story and placing the focus of attention firmly on the principals.

It is worth taking immense trouble with your opening paragraph, and especially with the first sentence. Make it intriguing, make us want to go on reading, get your hooks into us straight away. I have often asked my Creative Writing classes to look at two opening sentences:

The first is: 'Jane and Henry had lived all their married life in a three-bedroomed, semi-detached house.' Boring, isn't it?

The second is: 'Jane and Henry had lived all their married life in a three-bedroomed, semi-detached house, one room of which had remained locked since the day they moved in.' Well, it may not be brilliant, but at least most people would want to go on reading to find out why the room had stayed locked.

I should also like to suggest that there should be some kind of indication on the first page of what sort of book it is, so that if it were, say, a battered paperback copy without cover or title page, you would still know, soon after you began to read, whether you had in your hand an historical novel, a crime story, a romance, a contemporary novel or whatever kind of fiction it was.

All these points boil down to the same thing – 'the body on page one'. Between the two World Wars, the detective story, then at its height, would often begin with several chapters describing the manor house and the weekend guests, and the body would not be found in the library until a third of the way through the book. Another chapter would be spent on the guests' reactions before the great detective arrived to start the investigation. It was a more leisurely world. Nowadays we need to have the body on page one – literally, if it is a murder story, and metaphorically, if it is any other kind of book.

Originality

I suppose every writer wants to be original. It is seen as a key to success, and to some extent that may be true. But there is no harm in taking a model for whatever kind of writing you want to do, especially if you allow yourself to be influenced by a writer who is acknowledged to be a master of the craft. Of course you must not copy too slavishly, and your aim should always be to find something of your own to say, and a voice of your own to say it in.

As for devising an original plot, don't worry too much. The number of basic plots in existence is strictly limited, and the best that any of us can hope to do is to produce an interesting variation on one of them.

We can also try to use backgrounds that no one else has explored before, and we can experiment with narrative techniques and illumine our work with unusual and striking imagery.

But perhaps the best opportunity we have lies in characterization. Pour all your imagination into the invention of your characters, and if you succeed in creating new and interesting individuals, then, since everything in a novel stems from the people in it, you may perhaps have a valid claim to originality.

What Not to Write

Any subject under the sun can be used for a novel, but there are some elements which, unless in the hands of a writer of outstanding power, are to be avoided. My publisher has given me a list of his personal pet aversions, which I am sure are shared by many other fiction editors; he suggests that one should avoid: identical twins, amnesia, defecting scientists, arranged marriages/engagements, madness (to explain the irrational behaviour of the murderer), large chunks of travelogue material, religion, politics, children and animals (except insofar as the latter are concerned with children's books and books about animals). What have these elements in common? Some of them are clichés, others are boring or have no place in a novel, and others again will leave the reader feeling cheated because the author has used too much coincidence or has not provided a real solution to the central problem of the story. It's quite an exhaustive list, but it still leaves a million possibilities.

Endings

The end of this chapter is perhaps an appropriate place to remind readers that the ending of a novel needs to be tackled with great care, and a fault to be avoided is that of rushing it. Take time to let the reader off the hook, so that he doesn't feel hurried, and make sure that at least all the important ends of your plot are neatly tied off (though if you go too far in this direction, it may sound rather contrived). And whether your ending is entirely happy, or somewhat downbeat, make sure that justice has been done, that the central character has reached some kind of watershed in life, and the antagonist (or villain) has got his come-uppance.

8

The Novel – Characterization

Where do you Find Characters?

I am always rather surprised when would-be novelists ask this
question, and I wonder whether they should be attempting to
write fiction, or whether they would be better suited to
journalism or biography, working with real-life, ready-made
characters. But if you can teach yourself other aspects of the
novelist's craft, why shouldn't you learn where characters are
found?

Most successful writers of fiction would tell you, I think, that
their characters are formed partly from observation but most
often from within themselves. I have already suggested that we
all carry within us the seeds of humanity, which is why we can
find at least some understanding for other people, even when
they act in ways that are totally foreign to us. The psychologists
tell us that every man has a certain amount of the feminine in
him, and every woman something of the masculine; and there
are elements of both the saint and the devil, in varying degrees,
in our natures. The differences between us are simply due to the
varying intensities of our instincts and the degrees of control we
exercise over them.

So I believe you can find characters in yourself. James
Thurber's *The Secret Life of Walter Mitty* is not just an
amusing story – it says something true about human beings, and
especially about authors. Every fiction writer is a Walter Mitty,
though the dream-people into whom he escapes are not always a
total contrast to his own character and may be conceived in
much greater depth – perhaps even researched – so that there is
more reality and less fantasy about them. Imagine yourself into
the characters that you want to portray, just as actors do.

'But I have no imagination,' some writers protest.

I don't believe it. If you dig down inside yourself, I am sure you could imagine how you would react in various circumstances, and if you tried hard enough, you would also be able to imagine how members of your family and close friends would behave. You can do this because you know yourself, your family and friends intimately. Learn everything you can about your characters, and you will be able to imagine yourself in their shoes too. You can practise the technique by using well-known people. Take a simple incident such as breaking a favourite ornament and imagine how a famous person (the Queen, for example, or Arthur Scargill, or Steve Davis, or Esther Rantzen) would react if it were their fault – would they laugh, or cry, or be indifferent, or *pretend* to be indifferent? Try it again and imagine someone else drops the ornament; and again if that someone else is a person the owner regards as an enemy.

Of course, you can also take your characters directly from life, but most writers find the direct portrayal of a relation or friend unsatisfactory. You may not be able to manipulate a real person within your story as you would wish, and there is also the possibility of giving offence or even finding yourself with a libel suit on your hands. (I am not sure that I believe those authors who do work in this way when they claim that their real-life models rarely recognize themselves.) If you take a character from life, look at the person, as E.M. Forster suggested, through half-closed eyes, so that his characteristics are blurred, and put him into circumstances different from his own.

Most frequently, authors use composites, taking some character aspects from one person known to them, and other bits from another, perhaps blending several acquaintances into one fictional individual and nearly always adding a bit of imagination and something from within themselves.

Building the Character

You need to know everything you possibly can about your characters, even if much of what you know will not actually appear in the writing. It may be totally irrelevant to your story for the reader to know, for instance, that your heroine went to a comprehensive school, but you must know it, because it will help to make her real in your mind, and it may affect the way she behaves in certain situations. You don't necessarily put the fact in the story, but you do remember it yourself.

It is helpful to make a list of details about your main characters. Begin with facts such as age, height, weight, looks, colouring, build, address, occupation, habits, and continue with material about parentage, upbringing, schooling and experiences prior to the beginning of the story; then go on to the even more important personal characteristics, such as intelligence, attitude to life, opinion of self, relationships with others and so on; finally, add the character's aims and ambitions, in life and particularly in your story. This last is one of the most important influences – the more you know about the motivation of the people in your story, the better. When you have finished, you should have what amounts to a potted biography.

After doing this for the main character or characters, move on to the less important people in your story, and repeat the exercise. You need not go into quite so much detail, but whereas your main characters were probably already fairly well known to you when you started your list, simply because they are principals in your story, you may have to struggle a little more to decide just what those of lesser importance are like. However, their function in your story will probably largely dictate their characteristics.

How Do You Put Characters on the Page?

You can of course tell the reader about your characters when they first appear in your story, using all the notes you made about their physical appearance and background and characteristics, and pouring it out in one enormous slab of descriptive material. But this is not to be recommended. Even the physical appearance of your characters is better spaced out. Have mercy on your reader, and remember that there is a limit to the amount of information that he will be prepared to absorb at any one time.

Characteristics will be much more effective if seen rather than described. Character is in fact revealed in action or in dialogue. To show someone behaving bravely, say, or gossiping maliciously has far more impact than for the author to tell the reader that the person is courageous or has a bitchy tongue.

Very small actions can be indicative of character. A piece written for a Creative Writing class showed two neighbours having a cup of tea together, and the visitor, while talking, absent-mindedly broke off a piece of her biscuit and gave it to the dog; that one sentence immediately presented a picture and told us more about the character of the woman than a whole page of descriptive material would have done.

Character is also very clearly revealed in reactions, both actively and passively – actively when a character reacts to an event or to someone else in the story, passively when we see others reacting to him. Colin Wilson says, 'Human identity depends largely upon other people. We see ourselves reflected in the mirror of their eyes.'

Characters can also be established in the reader's mind by using some quirk of speech – a stammer, perhaps, or a habit of repeating the final words of sentences, or of echoing what others say, or by speaking in dialect or with an accent. But this and other similar idiosyncrasies are no more than aids, and in any case have to be used sparingly if they are not to become obtrusive (see page 89). They are no substitute for characterization through action and reaction.

Reader Identification

Readers like to identify with the main character in a novel, and this applies more or less regardless of the sex of the character. Reader identification is one of the most potent factors in fiction – all bestsellers, all great classics of fiction have it – and you, the author, have to make it possible in your book. How do you do that? Well, you have to engage the reader's sympathies, so in the first place your character needs to be sympathetic – a nice person, with admirable attitudes, and an aim in life which the reader will respect. That doesn't mean of course that he or she has to be a goody-goody – indeed, the odd human weakness will probably make the character more likeable. Let him have faults, let him lie (often very effective because of the dramatic irony), let him be human. It is even possible to get the reader to identify with someone who is really rather unpleasant, the key being a profound understanding of what makes him tick.

One of the best ways of securing the reader's sympathies is to make your main character the victim of injustice or, at the very least, misunderstanding. And it is here that one sees the value of a villain ('antagonist' is a better term) as a catalyst in the development of the story, and as a contrast to the hero, for whom sympathy will be aroused because of the antagonist's opposition. But remember to make such a person dark grey rather than totally black in his villainy – even baddies have some good qualities.

The main character needs to be strongly depicted, and also probably inherently strong as well. The so-called Gothic novel is usually centred on a young woman who spends most of the time in a somewhat unjustifiable panic, but even so apparently feeble a heroine normally has an underlying toughness, a strength of character which stops her from running away at the end of Chapter 1. And, moreover, these stories frequently introduce a genuinely weak character because of the excellent contrast this will make with the heroine. Yet another useful tip to be gained from a study of the Gothic novel is the value of placing a hero or heroine under stress in order to reveal his or her true character.

It is also of course a certainty that the heroine of the Gothic novel will win through in the end, and most people who read any kind of fiction want the central character to end up with at least some contentment. You may remember that Miss Prism, in Oscar Wilde's *The Importance of Being Earnest*, says of her own three-volume novel, 'The good ended happily, and the bad unhappily. That is what Fiction means.' A joke, but nevertheless it is what the majority of readers want in a novel.

On the other hand, stories in which the central character is a failure and remains a failure are very difficult to write (and publish) successfully – unless, perhaps, they are humorous. We enjoy the newspaper story about the rank outsider who wins the big race, but we may well not bother to read the details of an article headed 'X fails again'. In other words, we like to identify with winners, not losers.

Many writers tend to ignore humour, except perhaps for its use as comic relief, and do so mainly because they feel that it doesn't help to be funny when you are trying to build up the tension. But humour adds to the humanity and attractiveness of your characters, and so makes reader identification more likely. 'Laughter relaxes the characters in a novel,' says Henry Green, and goes on to add charmingly, 'And if you can make the reader laugh, he is apt to get careless and go on reading.' And a touch of humour stops a character from sounding over-solemn or pompous.

Character Development

In his book *Aspects of the Novel*, E.M. Forster speaks of 'round' and 'flat' characters. The reader does not need to know a great deal about the latter, nor to sympathize with them, and they exist to perform some minor function in the story rather than to engage our interest. They can therefore be presented with far less depth than the main characters, though this does not necessarily mean that they are weakly drawn, and indeed they can be very distinctive.

'Round' characters, on the other hand, are presented in much greater detail, and the author delves into and exposes to our view their motivations and emotions. Our interest and sympathy are aroused by the stripping away of the veil – that seventh veil which all of us normally refuse to tear away, even to our partners or closest friends. In a novel, the author strips his main characters of that last defence, so that we see all their innermost thoughts and motives.

There is, however, one other very important way in which 'round' and 'flat' characters differ from each other, and that is that the former develop and change. What we often find most fascinating about the people we meet in daily life is the way they are affected by circumstances. They change. Sometimes they grow. In the same way, we want the main characters in a novel to change and to grow, to end up better or worse, or somehow different from the way they began.

Names

It used to be possible to give the reader yet another clue to character in the names given to the people in your story – Jasper could only be a villain, Cynthia was likely to be a catty woman, Molly was jolly, and Christopher almost certainly a hero – but nowadays names no longer seem to carry these absurd instant characterizations, or not to the same extent.

Choose the names of your characters carefully, nevertheless. Make sure that you get the period right. Names go in and out of fashion, and if you are writing a period story, you will need to check that the names you use were in favour at that time. Even if your novel has a contemporary setting, the older characters in it will have been named according to the fashions of, say, fifty years ago. *The Guinness Book of Names* by Leslie Dunkling is immensely helpful.

Be careful to get variety in the names. If three of your main characters are called Janet, Jenny and Joanne, the reader may find some difficulty in distinguishing between them. I always try to name my characters so that their initials are different, and I choose some names which are single syllables (Jane, Tom), some which have two syllables (Sarah, Richard) and some – though there are fewer of these in popular use in the Victorian period which is my usual background – which have more than two syllables (Elizabeth, Frederick). The same rule applies to surnames, where again you need variety. I remember reading a war novel in which all the men seemed to have single-syllable surnames, several beginning with the same letter, which made it very confusing. The author altered them before the book was published.

Don't use names which are difficult for the average reader to pronounce. You may have some problems if your story is set in a foreign country, but even then it is usually possible to find names which are not entirely baffling.

As an extension to the last point, I think it is worth considering the euphony of the names you choose. Say them aloud, to make sure that they roll 'trippingly on the tongue'.

I prefer to avoid names which end in 's', because this obviates the awkwardness of the possessive version. Do you write 'Frances's' or 'Frances' '? Either version looks a bit clumsy.

Although names are no longer instant guides to character, they do still have some kind of identification in people's minds. I know, for instance, what sort of person I expect a 'Joan' or a 'Charles' to be, though my image of them is possibly very different from yours. But since most of us do have these feelings about names, it is worth taking quite a lot of time and trouble to ensure that *you* are happy with the names that you have chosen for your characters, that they seem to *you* to fit, because this will help to keep the essence of that character more firmly in your mind as you put him or her on paper.

A further point to bear in mind is that first names, as well as giving the reader guidance as to the period of the story, can often also indicate the social background of the characters. There may be many a Wayne and Darren and Tracy among the children of the wealthy and sophisticated, but most readers, coming across those names in a story, would expect their bearers to come from a much humbler background.

9

The Novel – Dialogue

The Function of Dialogue

The students who come to Creative Writing classes ask constantly about rules, hoping presumably that if they can learn enough of them they will be on the way to success, rather as if there were a Writing Test and you had to know your Writeway Code to have any chance of passing. I keep on answering that there are no rules, except perhaps those that I have set out in Chapter 18, and even they are no more than guidelines.

'Is there any rule about how much dialogue a novel should contain?' I was asked recently.

'No,' I replied patiently, 'but I suppose some other tutor of Creative Writing has told you that at least a third of a novel *must* consist of dialogue, or something like that.'

'Exactly that.'

'Oh, dear. It seems to me quite impossible even to suggest that such a "rule" must be observed. It depends totally on the type of novel you are writing, and on your own style and general approach.

'But watch people in a library or bookshop when they are choosing a novel. What are they looking for? If they are not stopping to read a passage here and a paragraph there but are just flicking through the pages, they are almost certainly checking to see that the book contains a good percentage of dialogue. So although there are no rules, I won't deny that dialogue is very important.'

Speech is the most common method of communication between human beings, and we like to find dialogue in novels because we feel we can depend on it to be easy to read and understand. It is also a simple, interesting and effective way of keeping a story going, and apart from the fact that its use can break up narrative passages which might otherwise seem too long, we expect a novel with a large proportion of dialogue to be fairly fast-moving. Finally, since it is so revealing of character, a large amount of dialogue assures us, if the author knows his job, of meeting interesting people in the pages of the book.

Writing Dialogue

The main problems in creating dialogue are to keep it in character, to make it sound natural and to impart liveliness to it. Many aspiring writers find these aims very difficult to achieve, perhaps because they somehow expect, since speech is so natural to all of us, that the dialogue in their books or stories will 'come' to them and that they will not need to work on it in the same way that they would expect to do with a piece of narrative.

The basis of effective dialogue is always to be found in strong characterization, and the more firmly you have drawn your characters, the more you know about them, the easier it will be for you to 'hear' them in your mind and then to transcribe their words onto paper. To some extent, your characters write your dialogue for you, and in that way, at least, it does 'come' to you.

But that is only a part of the job. Study the work of good modern playwrights, and notice how the lines of dialogue are kept always in character, varying in style according to whose speeches they are. If you look at them more closely, speaking them aloud, you will discover other things about them. You will see that they have a rhythm, that they are carefully chosen to advance the story of the play, and that they are extremely economical. And while they achieve all that, they also sound natural. The lines did not just 'come' to the playwright – he *worked* on them.

Natural Dialogue

Natural-sounding dialogue bears little resemblance to the way we normally talk. Tape-record an ordinary conversation, and you will find it is full of hesitations, repetitions, sentences which are unfinished or which ramble on without much consideration for grammatical rules or indeed facts; and there are interruptions, moments when more than one person is talking at once, sudden jumps from one subject to another, and so on. In short, a mess. The playwright, or the author of a novel or short story, has to edit his dialogue, so that all the confusing and boring bits are eliminated. The result is highly artificial. The dialogue in Harold Pinter's plays is supposed to be so natural that it sounds just like 'real life', but even that, when you examine it with care, turns out to be edited, selective, contrived (and those words are not in any way intended to be derogatory). Art may indeed hold a mirror up to Nature, but it is not an ordinary mirror; it does not reflect everything accurately, it emphasizes some aspects and plays down others, it controls what we see in it.

What we are aiming at, then, is not truly natural dialogue but something which sounds right because it is characteristic of the person saying it and which has a considerable degree of informality about it (unless the author intends the character to sound pompous and stilted).

In everyday life we tend to speak in fairly short bursts (often because someone else interrupts us), and enormously long speeches in a novel can seem very unreal. I think readers react to them with a certain amount of disbelief, just as they do when someone in a book writes a letter which goes on for a dozen pages or so. Of course, there are occasions in fiction as in real life when someone speaks at considerable length without interruption, and your long speech will be legitimate in such circumstances. However, even in those cases, it will be wise to break it up from time to time with a sentence describing some action ('He paused and sipped his tea') or perhaps the quality of the speaker's voice ('He was shouting now, almost screaming at them'), or something similar.

It is often possible to put the reader wise about essential facts by including them in dialogue, but remember that people do not normally tell each other things they know already. Let us suppose, for instance, that you want the reader to know that it is Lynne Smith's sixteenth birthday tomorrow. You could have a scene between her parents as follows:

'Don't forget it's your daughter's birthday tomorrow,' Mrs Smith said to her husband.

'Lynne's birthday? And how old will she be?' Mr Smith asked.

'Sixteen,' his wife told him, chuckling at his vagueness.

You might just get away with that if you particularly want to emphasize Mr Smith's other-worldliness, but it really is rather clumsy. Something like this might be better:

'Cosmetics! But she's too young,' John Smith protested.

'Oh, come on, darling!' his wife smiled. 'She's not a baby.'

'Were you using powder and lipstick when you were sixteen?'

'Of course I was. Long before that.' Mary Smith crossed her fingers to cover the fib.

'Oh.' He was momentarily disconcerted, but then returned to the attack. 'Well, I'll tell you this – she's not going to school tomorrow all dolled up with paint on her face, even if it is her birthday.'

Liveliness

As well as giving your dialogue a natural sound, you will want it to have vitality. Once again, strong characterization will be of considerable help to you. Firmly based characters will speak in their own voices (not always in your own), and you must make sure that they do so consistently. As you know, I am a great believer in reading work aloud for checking purposes; to do so is obviously of particular importance where dialogue is concerned, and it is worth reading all the speeches you have given to any one character one after the other to check that they are all in character. If the people in your story do talk in their own individual voices, this will provide variety and contrast in the rhythms of the dialogue and also probably in the length of the speeches.

You can also often intensify the liveliness, even if you are not using a totally naturalistic technique, by the occasional interruption or hesitation or repetition; or you can introduce wit or humour, though that may depend upon your own ability to be funny or witty; but everyone can manage lies, and they can be of immense value in dialogue. In the second passage of dialogue above, Mary Smith tells a small untruth. It may not be particularly sparkling, but it adds a little verisimilitude to the lines, because people don't speak the truth all the time. Nor do they necessarily always say what they mean. Talleyrand said, 'Speech was given to man to disguise his thoughts.' That leads of course to dramatic irony, which nearly always adds a bite to the dialogue.

Vitality can also be intensified in your dialogue by the use of emphasis, or the way you break up a speech with pauses, or the insertion of small pieces of narrative, or simply by the position you choose for the attribution (i.e. the 'he said' or 'she said').

Another factor which maintains liveliness is elimination of all dialogue which does not advance the story. Obviously, not every single line can be of great significance, since the seeming natural-ness of the speeches has to be maintained, but many of the gambits that we go in for in real life must be cut. Greetings, inquiries as to health and comments about the weather are commonplace at the beginning of many of our conversations, and we spend a lot of time asking people if they take sugar, and where they are going for their holiday, and saying things like 'Have I told you about ...?' or 'Last Wednesday – no, it was Thursday, because it was the same day as ...', and so on and so forth. Keep that kind of dialogue in only if it has some point in your story; the addition of two lumps of sugar to a cup of tea might be crucial to the action which follows, or it could be that another character's reaction to a comment on the weather is of importance (a line of dialogue spoken by one character always has an effect, or should have, on the person or persons to whom the remark is addressed). Normally, however, these everyday exchanges are so boring to read that they don't even manage to persuade the reader that the resulting dialogue is natural. Chop out all unnecessary chat.

Perhaps the best way of giving your dialogue the vigour you want is to cut it to the bone. Be careful not to cut so much that the dialogue becomes unintelligible or ambiguous, but that aside, make sure that every word is needed and is doing an effective job.

Putting Expression into the Dialogue

Dialogue in books suffers particularly from the lack of direct contact between the reader and the author, who cannot use a tone of voice or facial expression to indicate how a line of dialogue should be said. He can use adverbs, but more than a few soon become obtrusive, and he does have an ability to show emphasis, which is usually indicated by underlining (translated in print into italics), but I always feel that it is something of a failure to have to indicate the tone by means of adverbs or a stress by underlining, and though I cannot avoid them altogether, I will always try to make my intentions clear by the choice of words and their order.

The simple words 'He walked to the window', placed between two sentences of dialogue, lend a little extra emphasis to the second sentence or suggest additional thought. Notice too the effect you can gain from varying the position of 'he said' in the following three lines of dialogue:

'I shall always remember that evening,' he said.

'I shall always,' he said, 'remember that evening.'

'I shall always remember,' he said, 'that evening.'

Not only do those three examples differ in emphasis and therefore in meaning, but they have different rhythms. Rhythm is of great importance in giving vitality to dialogue, and since it is something which the ear detects much more readily than the eye, it is essential, I believe, to read your dialogue aloud to yourself. Indeed, read everything you write aloud to yourself, but especially your dialogue.

Dialect, Period Speech and other Special Effects

Many successful books have been written in heavy dialect, and historical novels abound in which all the speech appears to be authentic for its period; in general, however, it is wise to be very sparing with such effects.

Dialogue which is full of local words is often very difficult to understand, and if the author insists in addition on attempting a phonetic rendering of the pronunciation, many readers will give up. You may also run into trouble with confusion between apostrophes and inverted commas.

The problem with period dialogue is that, however historically accurate it may be, it may sound like 'Godwottery', a term used to indicate a phoney period flavour (derived, I imagine, from the line, 'A garden is a lovesome thing, God wot!', which gives the impression of having been written in the sixteenth century but in fact came from the pen of a certain T.E. Brown, who lived from 1830 to 1897). Of course, if you are writing an historical novel you must also be aware of the opposite danger of using obtrusively modern words, especially in the dialogue. Bad American historical novels seem particularly prone to it – I call it 'the "Gee!"-said-Leonardo syndrome' – but perhaps it simply seems worse to British eyes and ears.

There are some devices which you can use to convey dialect or a period flavour without irritating the reader. For instance, you can concentrate on the speech rhythms of the locality or period, rather than on individual words which belong to that area or historical time, using the latter only occasionally. And you can ask your reader to supply the local dialect or the personal mannerism or the period flavour for himself, and you do this by the use of descriptive sentences such as 'he said, in his broad Yorkshire accent' or 'She repeated the last word. It was a nervous habit, as though to reassure herself that she really had said what she meant', while in the case of the historical novel, the trick is to make sure that the period is well conveyed in descriptions of clothes, furniture, food, manners and indeed the whole action of the story, and to keep the dialogue as neutral in a time sense as possible, using neither archaisms nor neologisms.

He said, she said

Many beginners, aware that repetition is generally to be avoided, worry greatly over having to repeat 'he said' or 'she said' in their dialogue. It is a strange fact that, while a reader is usually very conscious of any other repetition, the majority will happily ignore the fact that 'he said' or 'she said' appears a dozen times on one page. He takes in the meaning, but the words themselves slip by almost as though they were not there.

It is therefore totally unnecessary to use a whole gamut of alternatives (although some of them, including such obvious examples as 'asked' and 'replied', are quite legitimate).

Especially to be avoided are those made-up verbs, forced into describing speech, such as 'he gloomed', 'she worried', 'he gritted'. And I have a personal dislike of the 'came the reply' type of attribution – 'came the swift rejoinder' is even worse.

If you do want to use alternative words, try not to do so in several succeeding lines of dialogue. 'Said' is a kind of neutral word that you can use over and over again; any of the alternatives is much stronger and therefore more likely to be obtrusive.

Moreover, it is not necessary to attribute every speech, provided that it is clear who is speaking. None of us enjoys the long stretch of dialogue with no attributions at all, and no certainty of which person is speaking. It is infuriating to have to backtrack and count the alternate lines of dialogue in order to work it out. But we can manage a few lines on their own, especially if they are strongly characterized, and if there are other ways of identifying the speaker – by allowing one of the speakers in a duologue to use the other person's name (e.g. ' "I saw you, Moira" ' – which tells us that it is not Moira who is speaking), or by the introduction of a narrative sentence (e.g. ' "I saw you." Nick went over to the window').

The last person named is usually assumed to be the speaker of the next line of dialogue which appears, but this can often be clarified by the way you paragraph your dialogue. It is preferable, I believe, to start a fresh paragraph for each person involved in talking to one or more others, but this paragraph can usually also contain any action attributed to that character:

'I saw you.' Nick went over to the window.

'You can't have done.'

'But I tell you I did.'

Moira lowered her eyes, and then looked at him pleadingly. 'Of course I can't stop you telling David,' she said, 'but I beg you not to.' In the silence which followed, she went over to the sideboard, and picked up the decanter. She changed her mind and put it down without pouring herself another drink. 'Please, Nick,' she said.

The words hung in the air. The clock chimed the half hour, as if to fill the awkward break in their conversation.

'I'm at my wits' end.'

In this example, since Moira was the last person mentioned, the reader will assume that the final line of dialogue is hers. If the author's intention is in fact that it should be Nick's line, he will have to alter it to something such as: ' "I'm at my wits' end," Nick said at last.' Or, if the line really is Moira's, he might add an unobtrusive 'she said' to make it totally clear, but this may be necessary only if it is the final line of a chapter; if the story continues in the same situation, it is likely that the next paragraph will move back to Nick, with an attribution to him.

Inverted Commas

It doesn't really matter whether you use single or double quotation marks, as long as you are consistent with them, and remember that if you quote something within a line of dialogue you need to use whichever kind of inverted commas you are not normally using. That sounds like Double Dutch, so here are a couple of examples:

'Do you mean by "a slight delay" that we shall be here for hours?' James asked.

"He said, 'I never done it, miss,' and I believed him," Mary replied.

Paragraphing the Dialogue

The convention which is most frequently used is to start a new paragraph for each person taking part in a conversation, but to include in that paragraph other material relative to the person who is speaking, and not to start a separate paragraph if that one person's speech is interrupted by narrative. An examination of the way the dialogue between Nick and Moira has been set out, beginning near the bottom of page 90, should clarify this point.

10

The Novel – Backgrounds and Research

Settings

At the time when Robert Louis Stevenson said, 'No human being ever spoke of scenery for above two minutes at a time, which makes me suspect we hear too much of it in literature,' it was fashionable to write at length about the physical backgrounds against which stories were set. Nowadays, it is generally the habit to keep descriptions of places, whether exterior or interior, and of climatic conditions, to the minimum, because readers recognize paragraphs which do not have a direct bearing on the plot and tend to skip them.

Of course, sometimes the setting is of considerable importance to your story or so interesting that it must be described in detail. Even then it is better, as with the physical description of your characters, to split the material up and give it to the reader in small, spaced-out fragments rather than in one large dollop. And it helps considerably if you allow the scenery or any other kind of background material to be seen through the eyes of your characters, rather than narrated directly by you, the author.

All this is not to decry the value of settings, which can be of great value in establishing atmosphere and mood. It is possible, however, to convey a great deal without going into much detail. My novel *The Silk Maker* opens in a room, the sole description of which is that it is dimly lit and silent, in a small cottage. The only other information the reader is given is that there is a hardwood chair and that a dozen or so books stand on the mantelshelf, but I believe that the reader will nevertheless have a very clear idea of what the room and the rest of its furniture are like. Why I am so certain of this, incidentally, is because I tried the experiment of reading the passage when it was still in draft to one of the Creative Writing classes I was taking, and then asking the students to write their own, fuller description of the room. Each produced a verbal picture almost entirely in accord with what was in my own mind.

Just as you need to know everything about your characters but do not have to include every detail in the text of your story, so you can get away with the minimum of description and still present a convincing background to your reader, provided that you know it fully yourself. I find it essential to visit the places where my stories are set, so that I can absorb something of their atmosphere, and since I am usually writing about a period of a hundred years or more ago, I eliminate mentally the high-rise blocks and the television aerials and try to visualize the countryside as it was.

Of course, you may want to use imaginary backgrounds, and there is no reason why you should not, or a combination of the real and the invented. But if you are creating a new house or village or town or even country, you should spend some time in working out exactly what it is like and probably making yourself diagrams or maps as appropriate. The object again is total knowledge, even if it simply stays at the back of your mind and never gets put down on paper.

The Background as an Integral Part of the Story

Backgrounds are not confined to scenery and the places where your characters live. They can also provide a much more important element in your story, usually in the form of the occupation or the milieu of your main characters. So you can have a novel with a political, industrial or underworld background, or the story could take place during an exploration in the Brazilian rain-forests, or while a bye-election is going on. And in each case, the background has a major effect on the characters, often supplying them with motivations and usually offering opportunities for the development of the plot. The basic theme may be simple and well tried – the rags-to-riches story, or boy-meets-girl-boy-loses-girl-boy-wins-girl – but its background causes it to develop in less hackneyed ways and gives it a veneer of originality.

My own novels all have an industrial background – wine-growing and making, for instance, or the manufacture of mourning crape in Victorian England. People often ask me if I have always been interested in wine or whether silk-making is in my family. The answer in either case is 'no'. I have always had to acquire the background knowledge and turn myself into an expert on the subject, at least while writing the book, and I have done this simply by research.

It is fairly easy to bone up on a subject, but you have to use your knowledge with care. It does not work to insert great chunks of background information without valid reason, and the details must be worked into the plot, so that they come across naturally. A very useful device is to have a major character who does not understand everything about whatever the background may be; it has to be explained to him, or he has to learn it, and that enables the author to put the information in front of the reader in an unforced way. Provided it really is relevant to your story, you can include substantial amounts of this kind of background material.

Research

'Write about what you know' remains good advice, but it is entirely possible to acquire a great deal of knowledge about all kinds of things of which presently you are entirely ignorant. There is a certain amount of hard work involved – you may need to do a great deal of reading (which should not be a hardship for an author), and you will probably have to find experts and persuade them to give you the information you need, and quite a lot of travel could be involved. You will almost certainly have to spend time in libraries or museums tracking down facts of various kinds, though you will possibly be able to do all the research you need simply by going somewhere and watching whatever it is you are interested in.

Where do you begin? You might start by making a list of what you need to know. Supposing you were writing an historical novel, you might want to find out what world events were happening at the time which would affect your characters, how a particular job was done and by what sort of people, how people travelled, what they earned, what they ate, what they wore, what the places where it all took place looked like at the time, and so on.

Having made your list, what next? I am fortunate enough to have an *Encyclopaedia Britannica*, and I always turn first to that, finding not only background material but sometimes something which actually affects my plot and characters. Before starting to write *Mario's Vineyard*, I learned from the *Britannica* about the vine disease phylloxera, which reached Italy in 1878, and it was that which fixed the date of the novel and also gave my hero his principal motive for leaving Italy to go and work in California.

Next I go to the library. The public at large thinks of librarians as the people who put a date stamp in the book when you borrow it and collect a fine from you when you bring it back late. But those are library assistants. Librarians proper think of themselves not only as custodians of books but as specialists whose expertise is the retrieval of information. Go to your public librarian, explain your needs, and you will almost certainly find him not only able to help but delighted to do so, and it will not be simply the resources of your particular local library which will be available to you but those of public libraries throughout the country.

Then there are the experts, and it is here that a curious fact comes into play. Although you and I know that authors are just ordinary people, to everybody who is not a writer they have a certain glamour. Go to your doctor with a cold, and unless he is very unusual he will barely bother to listen to your symptoms, but go to him (preferably not to the surgery but making a special appointment) and say that you are an author and you need his help, and can he tell you about this or that disease, and he will talk to you all night. Anyone who is expert in any subject likes to talk about it, and their willingness to do so usually increases enormously if they know that they will be helping a real-life author to write a book.

Equally, if you need information from some business concern, you will often find someone there who will be willing to show you anything in their manufacturing processes which is not secret, and to share their expertise with you. You can also visit museums, trade centres and the like. If you are writing a historical novel you should not neglect to read books written at the period which you are covering.

You can employ a professional researcher if you are short of time or unable to get to where the research material is stored, but you will miss much pleasure if you don't do it yourself.

Your Research is Showing

I suggested earlier that there was no limit to the amount of researched material that you could include in a novel, but I must stress that it has to be relevant to the plot, subtly introduced and presented in small doses.

There is a great temptation to a novelist who has discovered all sorts of fascinating facts about the period or the background occupation of the characters to put everything into his book, whether or not it really belongs there. If you do this, don't be surprised if an editor tells you that your research is showing. In my novel *Mario's Vineyard*, my hero had to walk on a day in 1879 from the railway station in Genoa to the docks; I discovered from research that a great town-planning exercise had gone on just before that time in Genoa, and I was able to describe the wide boulevards, the splendid new buildings and so on. But when my editor read the book, he said, 'What's all this travel-guide rubbish doing here? All you've written about vines and wines is there for a purpose, but this stuff has nothing to do with your story. Your research is showing. Cut it out.' And of course he was right.

Even if the material is essential to your story, you don't have to include it in one solid chunk. Diane Pearson says, 'Research is like manure – a little here and there makes everything blossom and grow, but in large lumps, it's horrid.'

You cannot read too much not only directly about your subject but around it. Immerse yourself in it. Know everything you possibly can. Keep detailed notes (which may be useful at a later stage if a sceptical editor, or even a reviewer, challenges your accuracy). But don't necessarily put it all into your book, and avoid especially the inclusion of anything which is merely peripheral knowledge. Simply bear it in mind as you write. It will give you confidence and lend authenticity to your story.

11

Short Stories

Before You Begin

As I have said before, the short story is one of the most difficult forms of writing, because it has to be precise, because it is restricted not only in length but in scope, and because it has no time to gather strength and speed as it goes along but must make an immediate impact on the reader. All this means that there is very little in the last four chapters on the novel which does not apply equally, or with even more force, to the short story.

It is of critical importance to get the construction right, to keep the focus of attention firmly on the principal character, to show rather than to narrate, and to keep the tension and suspense going from the first word to the last. You have little time to develop character, so you must know your people so well that you can pin them down on the page with great economy, and every word of your dialogue, and indeed of the whole story, must be there to do a job and must be the most effective word for that job that you can find.

For all those reasons, if you accept the idea of advance planning at all, you must surely agree that it is of even greater importance for the short story than for the full-length novel. Most short stories brought to Creative Writing classes have the common fault of being written too quickly, too easily, without enough thought beforehand.

If you find it quite impossible to plan before you begin to write (and this applies equally to the novel), what you are doing in effect is producing a first draft which in itself is a kind of plan. Unless you are very skilled, you will have to do a great deal of rewriting at that stage to make sure that the construction and all the other elements are as perfect as you can make them, and only after that will you be able to start the cutting, the re-phrasing, the polishing which is the normal part of revision.

The Three Basic Styles

It seems to me that most short stories fall into one of three categories, which I call the Tale, the Slice of Life and the Twister.

The Tale is the kind of short story in which the story itself is the most important element. It has a very distinct shape – an unmistakable beginning, middle and end – because it is usually concerned with some dramatic event. When you finish reading it, you do not find yourself faced with any loose ends, nor are you likely to ask yourself what happened thereafter to the people in the story. It is complete as it stands. The challenge in this type of story is first of all to devise a neat and interesting plot which can be presented adequately in a limited number of words, and then to control the construction with great care. Everything that needs to be there must be put in, and anything which is not relevant must be excluded, and in your anxiety to meet those objectives, you have to be careful to avoid underwriting, so that the result seems rushed.

The Slice of Life, on the other hand, is far less concerned with plot and far more with atmosphere and character. In skilled hands it can be extremely effective, but I think it is a dangerous form for beginners to attempt, because it is so much more difficult than it looks to bring it off successfully. It often doesn't have much story and ends inconclusively, and sometimes seems more like reportage than fiction. But it is very deceptive, and if you examine any successful example of this genre, you will find that it too has been carefully constructed and written and that it is not simply a moment of real life observed and put down on paper but has been shaped and moulded by the writer's art. Very often too there is a most powerful sub-text – that is to say, a part of the story which is never placed before the reader in so many words but which nonetheless he will recognize and understand as an integral part of what he has read. Often this is a kind of reversal of dramatic irony, with the characters in the story knowing something which has not been revealed to the reader directly but only by implication.

Many amateur writers, looking at examples of this kind of story and saying, along with Claire Rayner, 'I could do that!', fail to realize that it is not just a question of recounting an anecdote or some incident from their own lives. The Slice of Life has to be a *story*. It has to tell us something about its characters, and while there may not be room for a complex development, there must be at least some sense of change. It has, if you like, to have a purpose beyond mere entertainment – it has to reveal and illuminate.

The Twister is of course the type of short story which depends for its effect almost entirely on the surprise in the final paragraph or line. Everything else is subordinate to the twist ending. I think this is almost as difficult as the Slice of Life for the beginner to write successfully. The problem is always twofold: to produce a final twist to the plot which nevertheless arises directly from the characters and the situation, so that the reader does not feel cheated by it; at the same time, it must be a real surprise, which the reader has not been able to see coming. It needs considerable skill to build up this kind of story so that the reader is led along one apparently genuine path, as it were, only to find that he has been treading a different but parallel course. All too often, the unpractised writer has not exercised enough ingenuity in devising the story, so that it is either highly predictable or else a complete fraud, as when the startling final revelation turns out to be that everything we have been reading is in fact the principal character's dream. Oh, the numbers of bad short stories I have read which have turned out to be dreams! If you are thinking of using that idea, please think again.

Originality

In an earlier chapter I suggested that, if you were eager to be original, it would be better to concentrate on your style and on backgrounds rather than plots. It is worth striving for originality in these respects and in the high quality of your writing.

Although this applies to all forms of fiction, it is especially important if you are trying to write a short story. The point is that the reader is generally more critical, even if subconsciously, when he is confronted with a short story than when he has a novel in his hands. Because the whole of the short story can be comprehended comparatively quickly and completely, even minor faults become much more noticeable and can remain in his mind and tarnish his enjoyment of what he would otherwise consider to be a good, entertaining story. The little failures in a full-length novel, on the other hand, are quite likely to be overlooked and forgotten by the time he reads the last words, provided of course that the book has given him other satisfactions.

Originality in your short story will make the reader forget to be too critical. The alternative is to write with such care that he has little to be critical about.

Some Useful Tips

Remember that a short story is not just a greatly condensed novel. It is small in scale, so if your plot has lots of characters, and covers a long period and many different scenes, it is probably not suitable for a short story, though you may be able to develop it into a novel.

You have no time for a slow build-up of interest, but must hook the reader at once, so start at or immediately before a moment of crisis, and try to write a first paragraph which will make the reader want to go on.

Although you probably haven't got the space to allow the plot to keep twisting and turning, do try to include a surprise or two in the development of the story.

Once you have reached the climax, bring the story to an end as quickly as you can, and don't go into long explanations of what has happened or what will follow the events which you have described.

The Market for Short Stories

Writers who, like myself, are gently approaching middle age (along with Lady Dumbleton, of whom Lady Bracknell speaks in *The Importance of Being Earnest*, I have been thirty-five ever since I arrived at the age of forty, which is many years ago now) – writers with long memories constantly bewail the fact that the market for short stories has dwindled and indeed almost disappeared. Certainly, monthly magazines like *The Strand* have all vanished, and there is no daily or evening paper carrying a regular short story. As for collections of short stories published in book form (never popular with publishers, for the very good reason that they rarely achieve good sales), nowadays they are almost entirely confined to the work of very firmly established writers.

However, some outlets still exist. Chief among them, perhaps, are the women's magazines. The length required varies from about 1,500 to 3,000 words, and almost always the story should be centred on a young woman heroine. If you believe you can write for this market, it is vital that you should study it – buy all the magazines regularly over a long period, and check on the type of stories that they publish, their length, their attitude towards sex and marriage (whether, for instance, it is acceptable to write a story about a divorcée or to allow your heroine to live with a man without being married to him) and so on.

The so-called 'girlie' magazines also take stories. They do not necessarily have to be of a salacious nature, but they must appeal to the male reader. Even technical and trade magazines will sometimes print a short story if it has a relevant background.

Then there is the 'Short Story' (formerly 'Morning Story'), broadcast every weekday afternoon. The BBC is constantly on the lookout for good new writers for this slot. The requirement is for a story of about 2,500 words (the essential as regards length is that it should take just under fifteen minutes to read). Since it is listened to rather than read from the printed page, the story needs to be strong in plot (the Tale, rather than the Slice of Life or the Twister), focused on probably no more than two or three characters, and devoid of long and complex sentences which will be difficult to follow.

A specialist market for short stories exists in the Confessions magazines. They publish supposedly true-life stories, which are invariably fiction, though they may have their origin in genuine problems. The stories, which must be written in the first person, vary in length from 1,000 to 5,000 words. Since the magazines are read almost exclusively by young women with an age range of fifteen to twenty-five, the narrator-heroine has to be young. The basic formula is her confession of finding herself in some kind of trouble (not necessarily an unwanted pregnancy, nor indeed involvement in anything which she herself would consider sexually immoral) and of going through a period of unhappiness before solving or coming to terms with her problem – Sin, Suffer and Repent, in short. It is important that the heroine should find her own way out of her difficulty, though the ending need not be an entirely happy one – she can be left sadder but wiser.

Competitions

In recent years, perhaps because the market for short stories has dwindled, competitions for short stories have proliferated, and some of these offer publication to the winners. There is usually an entry fee – not an enormous sum but perhaps a consideration if you intend to enter a number of competitions – and you will need to enclose a stamped addressed envelope if you want your entry returned in due course. These competitions usually attract a large number of entries, so you will have to be pretty good to win a prize in them. It is not normal for the judges to give criticisms, so you may not get anything out of entering other than a long wait before the eventual return of your typescript. However, you never know. In one major competition with which I was recently associated, there were several beginners among the prizewinners, and a number of well-known 'names' who had submitted entries did not even get onto the shortlist. So it is always worth trying.

12

Non-Fiction

What It Takes

If your object is not merely to write a non-fiction book but to get it published, it is virtually essential that you should be either famous or an expert or an outstandingly good writer.

If you are nationally known, you will have no difficulty in getting into print. Publishers will probably come to you and ask you to write your autobiography; you won't even have to write it if you don't want to, or if you can't – the publisher will find a ghost writer (see below) for you. If yours is really a household name, you will be able to publish a book on just about any subject which takes your fancy; you don't necessarily have to know much about it, and again you won't have to bother with anything as laborious as actually putting the words on paper – signing your name on the agreement is all the writing you will have to do. Mind you, you may turn out to have produced what the trade scathingly refers to as a 'non-book', but you will be able to cry about that all the way to the bank.

Alternatively, you will almost certainly be able to find a market for a non-fiction book if you are really expert on your subject. In some cases publication may depend on your expertise being widely recognized – if you are writing history, for example, or historical biography, you will stand a much better chance of getting published if you are a history don, but this need for a national reputation (which is a much more serious matter than being famous) does not apply nearly so stringently if you are writing a school textbook or a book on embroidery or dog-training, so long as you really know what you are writing about and, though this is not vital, if you have something to say which is different either in content or form from what all the other experts in your field have put in their books. The one subject for which you need no smidgin of originality, to judge by the numbers of similar books which appear month in and month out, is cookery. Even then, of course, you have to know what you are writing about.

It is sometimes possible to overcome the handicaps of being unknown and of having no particular expertise (apart from a poet's eye and any other such gifts that your fairy godmother may have bestowed upon you) if you write prose of really outstanding quality. And in this instance, your greatest chance of success is with what are known in the trade as 'nostalgia' books – reminiscences of your childhood, when the countryside was unspoilt and young people were innocent and beautiful and life was simple and honest and golden.

If you can contrive to be not only famous but authoritative too, and to write like a dream into the bargain, your future as an author is assured. Except of course that you are clearly too good for this world and will probably die young.

Research

I said earlier in this book that you can often supplement your knowledge by research. But while that is true in the case of fiction, for which you usually do not need more than sufficient information to provide a background for your characters, and in the case of articles, which, because they tend to brevity, do not require you to delve too deeply, it is not true for the non-fiction book. For a factual book you really must have a solid knowledge of your subject.

Your expertise does not mean, however, that you will not need to do any research. Writing a non-fiction book is very testing. It demands far more than giving a series of lectures, for instance, although you may speak enough words in them to fill a book; and even if you are writing about something which is your life's work, you may find it much more difficult than you expect. A book is permanent, so you need to be accurate from start to finish. When you come to put everything on paper, you will probably find that there are aspects of your subject which you know slightly less well than others, and since you want every sentence in the book to be authoritative, there will be quite a bit of research to be done. You will also almost certainly have to check some of your information. You need find only one wrong date to begin to question everything you thought you knew so well, and you will then want to verify every single fact. At least, I think you will. There are some authors who don't seem to care too much whether or not they are accurate. That is an extraordinary attitude.

Ghost Writers

It is a fairly well known fact that many books which appear under the names of celebrities are not written by those persons but by ghost writers. Nowadays the existence of ghost writers is often admitted with the phrase 'as told to' or the word 'with' – '*My Story* by Famous Actress, as told to Joe Bloggs' or '*Play it My Way* by Famous Sportsman, with Joe Bloggs' (Joe Bloggs being the ghost writer, of course).

How do you become a ghost writer? To begin with, you need to be a special kind of person. The good ghost writer is able to submerge his own personality and absorb his subject's to such an extent that the reader will believe that these are really the words of the celebrity concerned – very often some of them are, because one of the ghost's techniques is to get his subject to reminisce onto tapes which he transcribes and edits. But you cannot do that work and provide all the linking material and present a reasonably true picture of the person concerned without either destroying his public image or offending him, unless you have a considerable sympathy for him and a great interest in and knowledge of whatever it is that has made him famous.

It is quite difficult to get this kind of work, and you probably need to know either the publisher or the subject to get started. It is likely, moreover, that you would have to convince both of them of your ability before you would get a contract.

Contemporary Biographies

An alternative to ghosting the autobiography of some celebrity is to write a straightforward biography. An aspiring author might say, 'I went to school with pop star Simon Swizzlestick. I've followed his career from the very beginning. I've been to dozens of his concerts. I've got every record he ever made. I've never had a book published before, but I'd like to write his biography, and surely any publisher would be interested in it.' Possibly, but there is an important question to be answered first: do you know Mr Swizzlestick well enough not only to approach him in the matter but to convince him that you are the person best fitted to write such a book? Only if he is adamant that you are to be the author is a publisher likely to accept an unknown writer who has no track record of any kind. On the other hand, if, despite not having previously written a book, you can point to a number of published articles, you may stand a chance. Even then you will need your subject's agreement and the ability to prove that you have an unrivalled knowledge of him.

All that applies, of course, whether you want to write about a pop star or a politician, an archaeologist or a zoo-keeper.

Translations

Perhaps your ambition is to translate books from one or more foreign languages into English. Normally, the translation of a book is arranged by the British publisher after he has bought English language rights from the foreign publisher. So it is not a question of getting permission to translate the books from its author or from its foreign publisher. If you know which publisher is going to bring the book out in English, you can write and ask to be considered as its translator, but it is more than likely that he will already have commissioned someone.

Your best bet is to offer your services (giving details of your qualifications, of course) to as many publishers as you can afford and be bothered to write to, and then wait in the hope that one day one of them will come to you with a translating job. You can also, if you wish, suggest to a British publisher that he should publish a translation of such and such a foreign-language book, adding that if he decided to do so you would like to be considered for the work, but there is no guarantee that he will adopt your suggestion or that, if he does, he will commission you to do the translation, unless there is some special reason for doing so, such as your friendship with the author, or your specialist knowledge of the subject.

How to Write Non-Fiction

In general, much of what has already been written in this book applies as much to non-fiction as to fiction. In particular, I think it is absolutely essential to plan a non-fiction book in some detail before you begin. List the headings for the various sections or chapters, or sub-divisions within chapters, making sure that you have included every aspect of the subject which your book is intended to cover. Then try to sort them into some kind of logical sequence before you begin to write.

It is sometimes quite difficult to arrive at a satisfactory order for your chapters. This book itself is a good example of the problems that may be met. It was easy enough to decide to start with generalities – the writer's needs, what to write about, planning, words and revision – and to continue with the 'specialist chapters' – the novel, the short story, non-fiction and so on. It seemed logical at first that material about the preparation of the typescript and thoughts on selling your work should come towards the end of the book, but then I thought that those two chapters really belonged with the first five, since they too were of general, rather than specific, concern. So I altered the order in that way. But then a good friend who read the typescript persuaded me that I should revert to my original plan (which just goes to show how useful it can be to have an outside view).

If you are writing a book which can in any way be described as instructional – not necessarily a textbook but one in which you set out to explain your subject – remember that you not only have to write simply, clearly, unambiguously, but must avoid assuming that your readers share your own knowledge.

This is particularly true if you are writing for beginners. Suppose your book is on how to play a guitar: the meaning of the word 'fret' is undoubtedly obvious to you, but it won't be to a complete beginner unless you explain it (or include a diagram on which it is clearly indicated). Of course, if you are writing for a more advanced readership, you will not have to explain so much, but the problem must still be borne in mind. When Stanley Doubtfire wrote his book *Make Your Own Classical Guitar*, he could perhaps assume that his readers would have some basic knowledge of carpentry, however slight, but once he had finished it he used his text as a manual, making a guitar by following the instructions in his book exclusively and to the letter. By so doing, he was able to tell whether he had included everything essential and had made everything clear, or whether anything in the book depended on prior knowledge which his reader might not possess.

You will also undoubtedly need to study your market in order to be sure that you are producing a book of the right length (and therefore price) and that the market is large enough to sustain the book.

Illustrations, Footnotes, Index, Permissions

A high proportion of non-fiction books needs to be illustrated or to have footnotes and an index, and if you intend to quote from the work of other authors or if you want to use illustrative material which you cannot originate, you will also have to think about the cost of obtaining the necessary permissions.

Illustrations are often expensive to reproduce, and unless they are an integral part of your book, it is probably advisable to wait until you have interested a publisher in the project before proceeding too far with them, but it is certainly worthwhile to have a list of the drawings or photographs which you would like to see in the book if it proves viable.

Footnotes nowadays are usually placed at the end of a chapter or even at the back of a book (because this saves a huge amount of money in the typesetting), which means that they are quite difficult to refer to. Of course, notes are essential in some cases, but if you can incorporate them into your text without getting bogged down in side issues, it is quite a good idea to do so.

The index cannot be completed until you receive printer's proofs, but if you compile it yourself, you can do the preliminary work at an early stage, using the page numbers of your typescript, which are then fairly easy to change when you get the proofs. If the index is likely to be extensive and complex, the publisher will probably wish to employ a professional indexer, and may ask you to contribute towards the fee. It is usually wise to agree, since indexing is far from being as simple a job as it may at first appear. (If you do intend to compile your own index, you will find that *Book Indexing* by M.D. Anderson gives much useful advice.) It is helpful if, when submitting the book, you can say whether it requires an index (and the same applies to illustrations, footnotes and so on), and if it does, whether you are prepared to compile it yourself.

Permissions to use copyright material must always be sought. The charges can be very high. If you intend to quote from copyright sources or to use illustrative or any other material which is protected in this way, you do not need to obtain the permission until a publisher has actually agreed to publish the book. At that stage, he will probably be willing to advise you on how to go about getting permission (basically a question of writing to the copyright owner or the publisher concerned and explaining what you want to use, for what purpose and in which parts of the world) and may also discuss the financial problems involved.

What Not to Write

There is nothing that you should not write for your own pleasure and perhaps that of your family and friends, but if your aim is publication, there are some subjects to avoid. You may have had the most fascinating experiences, and your friends may always be telling you, 'You really should write a book', but unless your life has been really extraordinary (in which case you will probably be famous, to some degree or other), you are unlikely to interest a publisher in your autobiography. It is almost impossible to generate enough sales for the life story of someone totally unknown – unless, I have already said, you write angelically or can get into the nostalgia market.

Don't expect to find a market for a book on a subject which is of a minority interest so small that a maximum sale would be of the order of two or three hundred copies only – a history of the Little Muckington Amateur Dramatic Society, for instance, or a biography of some obscure Elizabethan gentleman whose distinguishing feature is that he never did anything of the slightest interest.

Your local parson has just deserted his wife and children and gone off with a teenage drug addict, and the story has filled the gutter Press for the last three weeks. Surely there is a market for a book about it. No, there isn't – partly because it takes quite a long time to produce a book, and by the time it comes out public interest will have waned, and partly because that sort of nine-days'-wonder story rarely has enough meat to it to make a book. Topical books are always rather dicey unless the subject has some depth to it and there is a reasonable certainty that they will still be topical when the publishing process is complete and the books are actually in the shops. As a matter of interest, it usually takes at least nine months between the acceptance of a typescript by a publisher and publication. This time-gap can be and is substantially reduced on occasion, but to do so is expensive and difficult, and publishers are likely to be willing to do it only when the subject of the book is of really major importance and the expected sale will be large enough to justify the extra cost and trouble.

Please don't write funny books about moving house. Everybody's experience when moving house is traumatic and, in retrospect, hilarious. The subject is too hackneyed. So are most humorous or anecdotal books based on the author's own experiences. But don't let me stop you if you really are a new Richard Gordon or James Herriott.

Selling Your Non-Fiction Book

The one great difference between selling fiction and non-fiction to a book publisher is that you can often – not always, but often – get a commission to write a non-fiction book on the basis of preparing a synopsis and a specimen chapter or even simply a few specimen pages. In other words the publisher will give you a contract and pay you some money before you have actually written the book (though of course it will be specified that you have to deliver the completed typescript by a mutually agreeable date). Mind you, the publisher will also probably wish to know something about you and your qualifications for writing the book, and the more of an authority you are on your subject the easier you will find it to get a commission.

Naturally, you have to study your market before trying to sell your book, and you need to follow most of the directions and suggestions in Chapter 19. Your aim should be to find a publisher who brings out the type of book that you have written, though if he already has an exactly similar book on his list, you had better try elsewhere, because he won't want two. On the other hand, you will have found exactly the right place if, for instance, you have written a book on tulips and have picked a publisher with a strong gardening list but nothing about tulips on it.

This applies to biographies too, only more so. If you have written a biography of Mary, Queen of Scots, it is rather less likely to be accepted by any publisher if a new book on her has recently appeared. It is a different matter if it is approaching ten years since the last major biography of the lady came out, because of something known in the trade as 'the ten-year rule', which states that a new biography of a major historical figure can be successfully published, provided naturally that its author has something fresh to say, roughly every ten years. In any case, however, most important biographies are commissioned by their publishers from established authors (and this they may do five years or so after the last big book on the subject, which allows good time for the writing and publication).

When submitting a non-fiction book, or an idea for one, it is very worthwhile to give the publisher not only full details of your qualifications for writing it but any specialist knowledge you may have about the market for the book, what other books on the subject are already available (and why, of course, yours is better or more up-to-date), and your ability, perhaps, to get sponsorship for the book, or an introduction by a big 'name' or some kind of endorsement from an authority. Everything you can do like that will help your chances.

If you want more information on how to set about it, let me refer you to one of my other books, *Non-fiction Books: A Writer's Guide*, which covers the whole subject, in full detail, including information on the qualifications needed for writing different kinds of non-fiction and the approaches which are most likely to interest a publisher, as well as advice on the actual writing of a non-fiction book.

13

Articles

What to Write About

If you are going to write articles, in effect you are going to
become a journalist. Journalism is about people and about life,
and the journalist's job is to find out and inform. You need an
inquiring mind, and you could do a lot worse than to remember
Kipling's rhyme from the *Just So Stories*:

> I keep six honest men
>   (They taught me all I knew);
> Their names are What and Why and When
>   And How and Where and Who.

Themes for articles abound – there is always material to be
found in a hundred different subjects, ranging from royal babies
to peculiar hobbies, from local history to anniversaries and
issues of the day. Your chances of publication may be increased
by writing about something unusual, but the most mundane of
activities – 'Walking the Dog', to pluck one idea out of the air –
could be very successful if you have something interesting to say
and can say it in an attractive way. It's the old story – strive for
originality, but if you can't supply it in your subject, at least try
to do so in your approach and style.

You do not need a great depth of knowledge, but you must do
your research with great care, making certain that you get all
your facts right. You must be able to write with authority, and
you can only do that if you know a great deal about your
subject – indeed, much more than will actually appear in the
article itself. It should go without saying that the purpose of
research is to provide you with the background material from
which you write your own original article, but some beginners

seem to think that all they need to do is to copy out what others have written. Apart from the fact that you may infringe their copyright and be guilty of plagiarism, an article which is no more than a mish-mash of other people's thoughts and ideas very often sounds flat and uninteresting. You need (and this is of course true of all kinds of writing) to put something of yourself into it.

At the same time, you have to avoid putting into an article too much of yourself, in the sense of your own experiences and opinions. The essence of an article is that it is informative, but, unless the writer is very well known and has, as it were, a personal following, a general rather than a private approach is to be preferred. So you are unlikely to sell a day-by-day account of your holiday called 'My Holiday in Majorca', unless it is written with such charm and humour and from such an unusual angle that it will seize hold of the reader's imagination and retain his interest to the end (in which case, you will doubtless find a more attractive title for it). On the other hand, you might find a market for an article full of useful advice – 'Making the Most of Majorca', perhaps – which could be based on your own experiences, but which would not be full of 'I did this' and 'we did that' and 'then I ...', and indeed would hardly have an 'I' in sight.

It is best to write your article with a definite market in mind, so before you even begin you have to study many issues of various magazines and newspapers to see what sort of material each one publishes, and which of them would be most suitable for what you have in mind. As well as checking on the length of published articles and the amount of illustration used and similar technical details, analyse the editorial policy, try to discover what sort of readership is aimed at. Study as many publications as possible, and keep careful notes of your analysis. The more carefully you do your market research, the better chance you have of getting the right approach in your work, of knowing where best to submit it, and therefore of being accepted.

If you come across a good idea for an article, it may be possible to sell it to more than one type of magazine, rewriting the same material differently according to the editorial policy of the publications concerned.

It is quite likely that in the course of your market research ideas for other articles will occur to you, and it is worth remembering that magazines tend to have a four-year cycle, which means that you can take a theme from a four-year-old issue and rework it with some hope of acceptance, whereas you should not duplicate something which has been more recently published.

How to Write an Article

The first thing to remember is that you need simplicity. An article deals with one theme only, and since (at least if you are writing for a newspaper or a popular magazine) its length will probably be between 500 and 750 words, it is not the place for really complex ideas and arguments. On the whole, articles are read fairly rapidly, and if you try to put too much in, the reader is often apt to lose concentration and to give up. For the same reason, clarity is essential – make sure that everything you write says exactly what you mean it to say, and if there is the least ambiguity, re-word it.

The market for which you are writing will not only influence your choice of subject but also have a considerable effect on the style of any particular piece. If it is intended for the popular Press, you will have to use brief, simple sentences, for the most part avoiding sub-clauses and adjectival or adverbial phrases, and your paragraphs too should be short, consisting probably of not more than two or three sentences, even though this may mean dividing up the material somewhat arbitrarily. A less basic style may be preferable for a trade journal or a heavyweight newspaper or magazine, but even the most learned of journals will look more kindly on something which is visually attractive – long, solid chunks of type are off-putting, so again break your material into paragraphs, though in this case of course you will do so only when the sense permits.

The first words of anything you write are of vital importance, and especially so with an article. Look for an 'eye-opener' at the very beginning, something which will really grab your reader's attention and make him want to read more. It could be a question ('Are you descended from a Peer of the Realm?'), or perhaps a fairly outrageous or humorous statement ('Englishmen are the world's worst husbands' or 'My cat belongs to a secret society'). Those examples are rather 'down-market', but if you are writing for a paper or magazine which has a somewhat less popular approach, your opening still has to have immediate appeal.

Having decided on your opening sentence, which should make clear what the theme of the article is to be, move on to explain and develop it. But don't waste time with irrelevant background information or other introductory material – get down to brass tacks as soon as possible. When you reach this stage, I think you will find it of great help to have planned what you are going to say, perhaps using Winston Clewes' thirty headings technique (see Chapter 3) or at least making a list of your main points as they occur to you and then juggling them into an order which will allow you to progress from one to the other and which will lead you to your conclusion. That ending will probably be another 'eye-opener', or at least a brief but strong summary of your theme, or something which rounds it off, and the more firmly you have that final sentence in your mind as you write, the more easily you will be able to shape the article as a whole.

The Presentation of your Work

As with almost all forms of writing, an article should be typed in double spacing on one side of the paper only, and the paper should preferably be A4 size. The first page should be a cover sheet, giving the title of the article, the name or pseudonym of the author, his name and address, the number of words in the article and details of any illustrations required. Since you will not be offering to sell the copyright in your work, you can also put on this cover sheet 'Single Reproduction Only' or 'First British Serial Rights' (or 'First US Serial Rights' or 'First South African Serial Rights' and so on, according to the market in which you are selling the material).

On the next sheet of paper, type the title at the top of the page (unless it is for the American market, when it is usual to begin halfway down). The title should be neither in capitals nor underlined – remember that underlining always means italics. The bulk of your material follows, typed in the usual way, with good margins. Indent your paragraphs, but do not leave an extra line space between them. Subsequent pages should be identified by the title and page number – for example, 'The Presentation of your Work 2' or, more simply and quite as acceptably, 'Pres Work 2'. It is not essential to have the same number of lines on each page, and indeed it is quite a good idea to end a page at the end of a paragraph, if it is convenient to do so. At the bottom of each page, except of course the last, put 'more' or 'more follows' or 'mf'.

Selling Your Article

Assuming that you have done your market research and have written an article with a certain newspaper or magazine in mind, the most effective technique of selling is not to send your material in 'on spec' but to write first, giving brief but clear details of the subject and length of the article and asking if the editor would be interested in it. It is always a good idea to find out his name so that you can address your letter directly to him.

When you send the typescript of a book to a publisher, it is wise to enclose return postage, but with an article of two or three pages, whether you submit it on spec or after a letter of enquiry, it may seem psychologically a mistake to enclose an envelope for its return, suggesting that you are expecting to get it back. Better, perhaps, is to send it with a stamped, addressed postcard on which you have typed some such wording as 'We acknowledge receipt of your material entitled ...', followed by alternative sentences (e.g. 'It is accepted, subject to editing', 'We plan to use it in our issue dated ...', 'We regret that we consider the material unsuitable for us.'), which the editor can strike out as necessary. Of course, you will have to keep a copy of your article, so that if the paper or magazine does not accept it, you can retype it and send it elsewhere.

Even if you succeed with it, you may be able to sell the article again (Second Serial rights), since some magazines will occasionally accept material which has already been published elsewhere. In such cases, when submitting your article, you will have to say where and when it was first published. You can also, of course, sell your original article in a different market; for instance, if you have sold First British Serial Rights to a British magazine, there is nothing to stop you selling First American Serial Rights to an American magazine, though it is customary to inform the American editor that the British rights have previously been sold.

If you intend to write articles on a regular basis, it will be worth getting a printer to produce for you the cards referred to above. Indeed, printed letterheads, including your name as well as your address, will give a professional look to your correspondence. You might, by the way, consider adding your country of residence to your address, since this gives the impression that you sell your work internationally, as many article-writers do, in particular finding a ready market for their work in the United States.

Timing is of considerable importance, especially if your article is topical or is tied to some particular time of the year. Most monthly magazines work on a three-month cycle, so that at any given time there is one issue ready for publication, another ready for printing and the third in the planning stage. Therefore, if you have written something for Midsummer's Day, for instance, you need to submit it in March, or April at the latest. Obviously, these timings have to be adjusted for dailies, weeklies, quarterlies, annuals, but if you are in doubt, it is worth writing to the publication concerned and asking when they require material to be submitted for any given issue.

Many amateur writers believe that it is impossible to get an article accepted unless you are a member of one of the journalists' unions, but this is not so. Even the most tightly closed-shop papers and magazines will accept some non-union freelance work, and most magazines actually depend on freelance non-union writers.

14

Poetry

What is Poetry?

Hundreds of authors have tried to capture the essence of poetry in a few words, ranging from Samuel Taylor Coleridge, whose self-styled 'homely definition' was 'the best words in their best order', to the anonymous schoolchild (quoted in *The Frank Muir Book*) who said, 'Poetry is that stuff in books which doesn't quite reach to the margins.'

Here are a couple of dictionary definitions: 'The art of expressing in melodious words the thoughts which are the creations of feeling and imagination', and 'The expression of beautiful or elevated thought, imagination or feeling in appropriate language, such language containing a rhythmical element and having usually a metrical form.' Neither is really satisfactory, but it is extremely difficult to define poetry. When Boswell asked, 'Then, Sir, what is poetry?', Dr Johnson replied, 'Why, Sir, it is much easier to say what it is not.'

But Johnson was attempting, I imagine, to distinguish between poetry and its lesser stable-mate, verse, as they existed at that time. A difficult enough task, but the good doctor was not faced, any more than those who came after him for the next hundred years or so were, with the problem of free verse. The Victorians could look at a piece of writing and say, 'Yes, that is poetry – or, at worst, verse – because it rhymes and its lines have a metrical form.' Nowadays, however, we often come across what appears to be a piece of prose somewhat arbitrarily split into lines 'which don't quite reach to the margins'; the lines are often of irregular length and have no immediately discernible beat to them, and yet this is called poetry and published as poetry and acclaimed as poetry.

Well, is it poetry? I would say that it can be but isn't always. I should like to try a definition of my own:

Poetry is writing which illuminates some aspect of our world, in a way which strikes us as penetrating and new and unusual. It does this by selecting words and images for their power and value, and using them with the utmost economy. The words do more than simply supply their own meaning or evoke direct images; they are also so chosen that they relate to each other in various ways: they may echo sounds, more faintly than rhyme but nevertheless clearly, in something that one might call harmony; they may have a deliberately discordant effect; they may qualify each other in some subtle way, or contain allusions, or in combination give rise to different images than they could produce singly. By selecting the words so that they perform any or all of these relative functions, the poet induces the whole to mean more than the total of the separate parts – the words somehow add meanings and emotions and mysteries, in other words, lying behind and beyond them.

Poetry may be metrical and it may be rhymed, but these attributes are not indispensable; rhythm, on the other hand, is essential, though it does not necessarily have to be easily discernible or regular, but may consist of an essential rightness and flow and balance in the phrasing, and often in the echoes and contrasts of the actual sounds of the words. This rhythm should also be apparent in the way the words have been placed on the paper, and if you write it down as prose, it will cry out to be split again into the poet's original lines.

Poetry, Michael Baldwin points out, must *sing*. Moreover, it cannot be read without arousing some emotion in the reader, a sharing of what the poet felt.

I think that last sentence is almost the most important, and I would like to suggest that a rough and ready guide to the recognition of poetry is that you are moved by it. Dylan Thomas goes farther: 'A good poem is a contribution to reality. The world is never the same once a good poem has been added to it. A good poem helps to change the shape and significance of the universe, helps to extend everyone's knowledge of himself and the world around him ...'

It is not necessary to understand poetry to be affected by it. As A.E. Housman said, 'Even when poetry has a meaning, as it usually has, it may be inadvisable to draw it out ... Perfect understanding will sometimes almost extinguish pleasure.' I think he too was talking of that basic and essential stirring of the soul.

Another qualification I would make is that true poetry stays with you and grows for you. I do not mean necessarily that you will recall it word for word, but you will not forget your first impression, and when you come back to it, it will say more to you than it did the first time, and indeed you may never exhaust its subtleties and its imagery.

My definition of poetry is lengthy, and still quite inadequate. But it does apply to free verse just as much as to poems in a more formal style, and I hope it may help you to see that those random lines, irregular and apparently rhythmless, are sometimes indeed true poetry.

There is one final point to make. You will remember Hans Christian Andersen's story of the Emperor's new clothes. A great deal of rubbish is to be found nowadays masquerading as poetry and getting away with it because no one dares to say that it is nothing of the kind. I know I risk being lined up with those critics who dismissed Beethoven, van Gogh or James Joyce as talentless and who have condemned any poet since the beginning of time who has dared to experiment and break the accepted rules, but I stick to my guns. Don't be bamboozled by the label. If it claims to be poetry, give it a fair trial even if it doesn't look to you like poetry. Read it several times, aloud as well as silently. See if it illumines its subject, see if you can recognize any sense of rhythm, see if it moves you. If it fails the tests, don't be afraid to condemn it. It's more than likely that you'll be right.

Poetry and Verse

'Verse' is a confusing word. It is used in 'blank verse' and 'free verse' to describe forms of writing which may well be poetry. But when it is used in contrast to 'poetry' it usually suggests something lower in the literary scale, which does not meet the requirements which I dared to list above – something which does not illuminate, does not use words and images of great value, does not stir the heart.

Verse can also sometimes be said to use rhyme and metre and rhythm with far less discrimination than the best poetry does. It can get away with weak rhymes, near rhymes, repeated rhymes, and it can use very marked tum-ti-tum-mi rhythms and such obvious metres as:

> di-dah, di-dah, di-dah, di-dah,
> di-dah, di-dah, di-dah,
> di-dah, di-dah, di-dah, di-dah,
> di-dah, di-dah, di-dah.

Of course, there is nothing wrong with verse. It is an extremely suitable medium for satirical and humorous work, and the sort of narrative that turns into a ballad, and there are many examples of English verse which are as immortal, if not as great, as much genuine poetry. The problems for the would-be writer arise when the demands of rhyme and rhythm force him into awkward wording, as for instance in the following absurd example:

> I wandered o'er the boundless lea,
> Where grasses high there were,
> And, oh, what joy when I did see
> A small bundle of fur.

Nobody would write quite as badly as that, but I have made up those four dreadful lines because each one illustrates one of the faults that are frequently found in amateur poets' work.

In the first line, we have the words 'o'er' and 'lea'. Nothing wrong with them, except that beginners feel bound to use such words because they are 'poetic', and that is usually a mistake. Some great poets have written in a deliberately precious style, but most of them have used contemporary language. Don't use 'poetic' words unless they really say more than something more straightforward and modern.

The second line is a typical double inversion. It should really read: 'Where there were high grasses', but that won't rhyme and sounds very prosaic, so the poet twists the order of the words to make them fit, but succeeds only in sounding clumsy.

'When I did see' – one meets this construction time and time again – 'I did go', 'I did tell' etc. The unnatural phrasing is used because 'I saw', 'I went', 'I told' do not rhyme with a line already written, and do not scan either. It never seems to occur to those who write in this way to change the rhyme by rewriting the previous line, or that some more acceptable way of achieving the desired number of syllables can be found.

The final line has that unfortunate word 'bundle', which here has to be pronounced 'bun*dle*' if the strong scansion is to be maintained. Especially when a very simple metre is used, which tends to emphasize such faults, it is important to search for and find words which will not disturb the rhythm. And if you fail in such a search, then you have to abandon those words and rewrite the line in some form which will scan.

The Writing of Poetry

It always seems to me more presumptuous to try to give advice to poets than to any other kind of writer. If you are a poet, you probably write naturally, and you won't need anyone to tell you how to do it.

That is not to say, however, that you should rely entirely on inspiration, or that because the work stems from your heart and soul there is no need to involve your head. If you look at the manuscripts of great poems of the past, you will see that the poet has usually done a considerable amount of work in revising and rewriting before he has produced the version which has become so familiar to us. No form of writing is more exacting than poetry, and the greater trouble you take, the more likely you are to succeed. Be critical of your work, and revise and revise and revise. Get the language and the rhythms right, avoid clumsy inversions and phrasing, and add as much polish as you possibly can. You may protest that this approach will result in something lacking in life and colour and excitement, but listen to

Kathleen Raine: 'Uncontrolled poetry has no character – and carefully worked-on poetry seems spontaneous and has style.' It's truer than you might at first believe.

Supposing you don't feel yourself instinctively to be a poet – does that mean that you should not attempt it? By no means. The last thing I want to do is to discourage anyone who wants to write poetry. But it *is* undoubtedly the most difficult form of writing, and especially if in your early efforts you find yourself very prone to the kind of faults that I indicated above in the section about Verse, perhaps you should ask yourself whether you would not do better with prose. To be a poet is a great gift which is not received by many.

Selling Your Poetry

It is notoriously difficult to find a general publisher who is willing to publish poetry other than that by well-established 'names'. A few of them will from time to time take on new poets, but you have to be both very talented and very lucky to get on their lists. On the other hand, many small, independent presses are devoted exclusively to contemporary verse, and several small poetry magazines are published.

Markets also exist for single poems. Various commercial journals (*The Lady, Country Life*, some of the women's magazines) occasionally take a poem, and trade or professional journals will also do so if the subject is appropriate for them or if you belong to the organization they serve. Local newspapers will sometimes print poetry, and though one always feels that their reason for doing so is simply to fill an otherwise empty space, it might even be worth asking the editor of your neighbourhood paper to consider a regular 'Poets' Corner'. You might also have the pleasure of seeing yourself in print if you submit poems to the local church magazine, even if you don't get paid.

It is usually best not to submit more than three poems at a time, wherever you are sending them. If the editor likes your work, he will ask to see more. Follow most of the suggestions in Chapter 19 on the submission of typescripts, but note that while poetry should be typed, it is not usual to use double spacing.

Type it, in fact, in exactly the same way as you would like to see it appear in print.

(Its physical shape can, of course, be an important element in a poem, and its visual impact can add to its effect. But do make sure, if you use a somewhat eccentric layout, that it is more than a merely arbitrary division of the lines.)

Publishing Your Own Poetry

Many poets, despairing of getting other people to publish their work, decide to do it for themselves. This may be vanity on their part, but it is not necessarily what is meant by Vanity Publishing (see Chapter 19). The best way of doing this is to go to local printers and get them to quote you for the production of however many copies you think you will want. The more you have, the cheaper each copy will be if you are looking for something which is actually set up in type. There will be less difference for quantity if you go to one of the print shops and get them to reproduce your work from typewritten copy.

Once you have produced copies, you can sell or give them to your friends. You can also try to persuade your local bookseller to stock and sell copies, but of course he will expect to take a percentage of the moneys he receives, so you will have to price the book accordingly. Remember that you should declare all such dealings to the Inland Revenue, and that you will be liable to tax on any profits that you make.

Further details on publishing your own work are to be found in *How to Publish your Poetry* by Peter Finch, published by Allison & Busby.

15

Stage Plays

Dialogue

A play is in many ways very similar to a novel or a short story, and almost everything that I have written on those subjects applies to plays, as does much of the more general material in this book. The difference between fiction and drama is simply that in a play the story has to be told almost exclusively through dialogue.

Some contemporary dramatists write formal, stylized plays, often in verse, in which they make no attempt to provide dialogue which sounds like everyday speech. But generally speaking, the current convention is for naturalism, and this applies even if you are writing a period piece. The language used may be archaic, but the aim is still to make it sound as though real live people would say it in just that way. We have already seen in the chapter on dialogue that even the work of Harold Pinter, supposedly the prime exponent of totally natural speech in drama, is carefully selected and edited. It may be the nearest thing we get on the stage to the chaotic way in which most of us talk, but it isn't completely realistic and would be very boring if it were.

Of course, one of the reasons that it does not work simply to transcribe a tape-recording of an everyday conversation is that much of what we say on such occasions is completely trivial and repetitious and inconsequential. Every line in a play, on the other hand, needs to be there because of its meaning and its contribution to the overall plan.

That brings me back to my hobbyhorse of planning, but before I move on to that, there is more to say about dialogue, and I particularly want to emphasize the fact that the speeches you give to the characters will be spoken aloud. That may sound absurdly obvious, but many aspiring dramatists write too much for the eye and not enough for the ear. When writing a play, you must speak the lines aloud, or at least 'hear' them within your mind, if only to make sure that they can be said and so that they mean what you want them to mean and nothing else. Perhaps my own meaning here will be clearer for a couple of examples. Both come from a rather dreadful Nativity play written by an amateur. It contained two memorable lines: 'Go and fetch fresh straw to strew in the manger' and 'I have travelled here with this merchant'. The former is not too bad on paper but is far too clumsy a tongue-twister to be spoken easily, while in the latter the words 'this merchant' tend to sound like 'this bloke' rather than 'this gentleman who is engaged in commerce'.

Try to ensure too that your dialogue has rhythm, by which I mean that easiness of flow, that rightness in the phrasing which makes us feel as we listen to it that it could not have been said in any more effective way. And, of course, it is absolutely essential that it should be in character. One of the tests of good dialogue is that if you cover up the names of the characters you should still be able to tell most of the time which of them is speaking, because their lines will have an individuality of their own. You must be careful to let your characters speak for themselves – don't have them all using your own voice, as it were – and the best way to achieve that effect is to know your characters inside and out, to have created them so strongly, so fully in your mind that you know exactly how they respond to any situation.

Dialogue is of course a matter of cut and thrust or parry, or it is like a pair of tennis-players hitting a ball back and forth across the net. In other words, once a conversation has begun, it continues in a series of responses. Just as the tennis game begins with someone serving, so the dialogue in a play is initiated by one of the characters, and the direction that it then takes is dictated by the responses to each speech and, please note, by the thoughts behind the spoken words. That last point is important – we normally think before we speak, except in the most trivial of exchanges, and the characters must think too. They need not necessarily express all their thoughts, but the audience should be able to guess what they are thinking, and this can be particularly effective when it is clear that their thoughts and what they say are totally at variance with each other.

If you are going to write natural dialogue, or what passes for it, you will obviously use shortened forms like 'can't' rather than 'cannot' or 'I'm' rather than 'I am' (unless the character concerned speaks more formally or the context demands the full version, which is usually a little more emphatic). But what about slang, and those meaningless phrases like 'you know' that we often use without thinking, and swear-words? The answer is that you use them as your characters would – with the one proviso that they should be intelligible to the audience and should not bore or shock them (unless it is your intention to shock).

Action

Not everything that happens in a stage play is spoken. Some parts of the story are told in visual action, and the importance of this aspect is perhaps indicated by the fact that we go to 'see' a play rather than just to listen to it. A stage play rarely works if it only presents people sitting and talking, nor is it enough to give them directions to move about the stage unless there is some good reason for them to do so which will also advance the story or add to the drama. It is also vital that important parts of the play should not take place off stage. If you do that, the best you can usually manage is for one of the characters to report what happened to the others, and that is not nearly so exciting or even interesting as seeing it before one's eyes.

You do not need to write in stage directions unless the movements are an essential part of the action. You may have to say 'They kiss' or 'She stabs him', but you do not necessarily put in 'He walks to the window' or 'She sits in the armchair down centre'. Movements which are made simply to present a good visual picture to the audience are usually left to the director of the play to arrange. It is also noteworthy that descriptions, when they first appear, of the characters and the way they behave should be unnecessary – it should all be clear from their actions and dialogue in the play. Equally, although you may wish to state the character's age, and there may be good reason for specifying the clothes that person is wearing, you should avoid physical descriptions, unless again it is an essential part of the play for the character to be exceptionally tall or fat or disfigured or disabled or whatever.

The Unities

For several centuries the theatre shackled itself with a set of rules which arose, with a certain amount of misinterpretation, from Aristotle's *Poetics*. These rules were the Unities – the unity of action (a play must have only one plot), the unity of place (there must be no more than a single setting) and the unity of time (the whole action had to take place in twelve or twenty-four hours). The rules are rightly disregarded nowadays, but nevertheless there are some practical aspects to them which may be worth considering.

The most important of the three rules was the one which demanded a single plot. It might seem that it is still in effect today, for in the one-act play there is generally too little time to develop more than one story or theme, and while a full-length play may have one or more sub-plots, these are usually closely connected to the main story. However, in the past the unity of action rule was followed so rigorously that the main plot tended to be very simple and straightforward, whereas nowadays we expect a considerable complexity in a full-length play, even if there is only one main theme – we look for a development, an exploration. And of course we are not restricted in subject in any way.

Turning next to the unity of place, it has to be admitted that the theatre has certain limitations – it cannot move from scene to scene with the freedom of film or television (or the much greater freedom of radio) – and though some successful plays do consist of a large number of scenes with different backgrounds, these often present a number of difficulties and cannot readily be staged because of the cost of the scenery and the mechanics of changing it, unless the audience is willing to supply the settings solely in their imagination (their readiness to do so is often exploited in theatre-in-the-round). But on the whole you are more likely to be successful, especially in the amateur market, if you can limit yourself to one or two fairly simple settings.

There is no need at all to restrict yourself as far as the unity of time is concerned, but this is perhaps the occasion to make the point that an episodic play in which there are many short scenes is much more difficult to write and perform successfully than one which is simply divided into two or three acts. The reason is that, every time you bring the curtain down or close it or black out all the stage lights, the audience loses at least a part of its concentration, and the playwright and the actors then have to fight to get it back at the beginning of the next scene. This is particularly true of the one-act play, for which the Unities can often be strictly applied to advantage.

The Unities did not have anything to say about the size of the cast, nor about the balance of male and female characters. In the professional theatre you are more likely to be successful with a cast of not more than six or eight characters, and this will probably work well for the amateurs too. To have only one or two characters may be attractive to West End managements but is likely to be far less so to repertory companies and to amateurs. And on the whole you need to be well established or to have written a real corker of a play to get away with a large cast. One cannot really generalize about the numbers of men and women in a play as far as the professional theatre is concerned, but the average amateur company has more women members than men, and that is worth bearing in mind.

The one-act play is largely of interest to the amateurs, and in addition to mixed-cast plays there is a steady demand, particularly from Townswomen's Guilds and Women's Institutes, for good one-acters for all-women casts.

Construction

In days when successful full-length plays were always divided into three acts, it was easy to lay down the law about their construction: Act I was Exposition, Act II was Development and Act III was Resolution. Nowadays, more and more often it seems that playwrights (or is it theatrical managements?) prefer the two-act form. Shakespeare wrote, of course, in five acts, and the four-act division has also been much used. It doesn't really matter – you still need an exposition, in which the characters and their situation and the theme of the play are presented to the audience, and you follow it with a development, in which you explore the twists and turns of the plot, all of which arise directly from the exposition, and finally you come to a resolution, in which you work towards your ending, whether it is happy or unhappy, whether it ties up every loose end or finishes in ambiguity.

Another way of expressing it is that you face your characters at the beginning of the play with a conflict of some kind – conflict is the essence of drama – and then show us how they react to that situation and to each other, and you end at a point when something has changed as a result of their experiences.

Construction is not, however, simply a matter of deciding on your exposition, development and resolution. You need also to look in more detail at the shape of your play, which is going to be a curve rising to its highest point at or just before the final curtain. It is not, however, an entirely smooth curve – there will be peaks and troughs along the way, and they need to be carefully planned. You will find Winston Clewes' thirty points system helpful yet again, and the advice about where to begin a novel or short story – just before a crisis point – applies equally to plays.

One word of warning about the ending: avoid the *deus ex machina*. This term, derived from the Greek theatre, means a character who arrives at the end of the play, having had no previous connection with the action, to sort out all the problems. For example, if your play is about a family's financial difficulties, it is not at all satisfactory to solve them by introducing in the last act a rich relative from Australia of whom no one has heard before. The ending must develop directly from what the audience has already seen.

Technique

If you want to write for the theatre, you need to learn something about theatrical technique, and the best way of doing this, unless you are a professional already, is by joining an amateur group. Don't despise the amateurs – many maintain a high standard, and even should you find yourself in one of the less capable societies, if you keep your eyes open and study what goes on seriously you will learn a great deal. By taking part in a play, or directing it, or working backstage, you will see more clearly how plays work, how playwrights get the characters on and off stage, how they give the audience any essential information, how they arouse interest and excitement. Moreover, your amateur friends may agreed to put on your plays, or at least to give them a reading, and that, as I have suggested earlier, is invaluable. It is astonishing, and I speak from personal experience, to find how obvious necessary changes become when you hear the lines spoken by other people.

The Market

If you want to write for the professional theatre, you will almost certainly need to use an agent (names of those who specialize in plays are listed in *The Writers' and Artists' Yearbook*), though if you have written the play with a certain star in mind, it is possible to send the play direct to the actor concerned. In either case a preliminary letter of enquiry is advisable, and you should enclose postage for the return of your typescript. For the amateur theatre, the market is virtually limited to a few publishers (notably, of course, Samuel French) who bring out what are known as 'acting editions', though some playwrights manage to sell duplicated copies of their plays through the columns of specialist magazines such as *Amateur Stage*.

As always, work should be typed on one side of the paper only, and preferably using A4 paper. As each character speaks, type his or her name in full and in capitals on the left-hand side of the page. The dialogue is typed in single space, but with a double space between the speeches of different characters. Stage directions are put in brackets and underlined. The following example will make that clearer:

ALGERNON: Cecily! (*Embraces her*) At last!

JACK: Gwendolen! (*Embraces her*) At
                    last!

LADY BRACKNELL: My nephew, you seem to be
                    displaying signs of triviality.

JACK: On the contrary, Aunt Augusta,
                    I've now realized for the first time
                    in my life the vital Importance of
                    Being Earnest.

16

Radio, Television and Films

Radio

If you want to write for radio, there are many possibilities open to you. You can write a short story, a feature, a talk, a poem or a play, and you can aim your work at different age groups and at interests ranging from the pop to the highbrow. The one limitation, if you are to stand any chance of success, is that you must write whatever it may be with the express intention of having it broadcast. Yes, of course published books are read on the air, and so are stories which were written first for magazines, but these are usually by well-known writers and, more importantly, they have nearly always been 'adapted' for radio.

The point is that most writing is meant primarily to be read, not listened to, and you therefore have to make sure in work intended for radio that all your words are clear and readily understandable, that your prose flows easily, that you have avoided repetitive rhythms (and more obvious repetitions), that you have included nothing with any resemblance to a tongue-twister and, in respect of drama, that you have not at any point relied on something visual to get your story across.

The BBC publishes a handbook, *Writing for the BBC*, full of helpful advice on the type of work which may be accepted for broadcasting, and it gives details of the various departments and their interests, and the lengths of material required and so on.

Talks are usually given by people who are authorities on a given subject, but if you have a really unusual personal experience to relate and can put it over with nostalgic charm, perhaps, or warm humour, or a certain amount of passion, you may find that there would be a slot for it on a programme like *Woman's Hour*.

In Chapter 11 I have already discussed the 'Short Story', which is the main outlet for straight fiction on BBC radio, the serials which are broadcast being taken most often from published books.

It should be remembered, however, that Radios 1, 2, 3 and 4 and the World Service – the main BBC programmes – are not the only programmes available to writers. The BBC handbook draws attention to the BBC's own regional stations and explains their requirements, but there are also the independent stations, many of which are fairly hungry for material.

Radio Drama

Although in some ways you are restricted – facial expression and movements of the actors are invisible, and it is almost impossible to convey in sound alone the 'business' which is the staple fare of farce and can be very important in other types of play – nevertheless, the freedoms which radio drama gives you easily outweigh its limitations. Scenery does not have to be constructed and put in place – all you need is a background sound or for a character in the play to say where he is, and the listener is immediately transported there (provided, of course, that you and the producer of your play have both done a good job). That is the great thing about radio – you have the asset of an audience which is not only willing but eager to lend you its imagination, for you to play on in any way you think fit. Moreover, because the transition from one scene to another can be so swiftly and clearly accomplished, there is far less need to pay any attention to the unities of time and place than there is for a stage play. You can go where you like, provided always that what you write is clear to the listener.

I must emphasize this point about clarity – if what you write is available in some form to be read, then the reader can read it slowly if he wants to, or go back over a passage that he doesn't quite understand, or turn back several pages to check some point that he does not remember. None of those options is open to him when listening to the radio, so he must grasp everything necessary to an understanding of the piece at that fleeting moment when he hears it. That may suggest that radio material has to eschew subtleties and complexities, but we all know that this is not necessarily so – all it means is that extra care has to be taken over clarity.

One of the restrictions you will meet in radio drama (and indeed it applies in virtually all writing for radio) is that everything must fit into a time-slot. If you write a novel, it can be of any length from 20,000 words (though we usually call that a novella) to over a million words (which we may regard as a doorstop); a full-length stage play will run for something between two and three hours, including the interval(s), and nobody is going to worry, give or take a quarter of an hour. But for radio everything has to be precisely timed. Radio plays fit into slots of varying lengths: 30, 45, 55, 75 or 90 minutes. You need to aim as carefully as you can at one of these lengths. How will you know how long it is? Read it aloud, and time it.

When you come to submit a radio drama to the BBC, you should put on the cover which length slot you intend it for, since there are different editors for the different length plays. *Writing for the BBC* tells you how to lay out the pages of a radio drama, but a clearer indication is obtainable by sending a stamped addressed envelope to the Script Editor, Radio Drama Department, Broadcasting House, Portland Place, London W1A 1AA and asking for a copy of 'Notes on Radio Drama'.

A curious thing about submitting plays to the BBC is that it is no use sending to one of the regional stations a play which has been seen and rejected by the BBC Radio Drama Department in London, but it is sometimes possible to do it the other way round, if you see what I mean. It is best in the first place to send a play to one of the regions only if you live in that area or if the play is very firmly set there. It is even more curious that once you have submitted a play to the BBC you will have to wait three to four months for a verdict, which seems an unnecessarily long time, however many submissions they receive.

Television and Film

Although *Writing for the BBC* devotes quite a lot of space to television, in fact you will be extraordinarily lucky if you break into this field without having first established yourself as a writer in some other direction, and you will almost certainly need to be represented by an agent. This applies as much to ITV as to BBC TV. It may be worth your while to try the less monolithic independent companies, but your chances are slim. However, talent and determination may get you there in the end – after all, those who write the plays and situation comedies and serials which appear on our screens so regularly had to start somewhere, and maybe you will be lucky. Dream up a really original and funny sit-com, and your fortune will be made.

It is probably even more difficult to become a screenplay writer for the cinema. If that is your ambition, I would suggest that you cultivate the friendship of a film producer, or alternatively become a bestselling novelist (since if you really reach the top of that particular tree it appears to be fairly easy to hop across to the highest branches of different trees). One other solution is suggested by the fact that cine cameras and video cameras are readily available and widely owned – so why not write a screenplay for an amateur drama group (and maybe produce and direct the film into the bargain)?

17

Writing for Children

The Easiest Form of All?

Most parents (especially mums) whose lisping infants demand a change from the stories usually read to them (or who can't stand the thought of going through the same old thing again) find it comparatively easy to make something up. All that is required is to put your small listener or listeners at the centre of the story, and relate some quite ordinary experience that has actually taken place. So you begin, 'Once upon a time there was a little boy called Wayne, and one morning he went shopping with his Mummy ...'. Alternatively you tell a story about animals, making them speak and behave like human beings: 'It was after seven o'clock when Mr Mole woke up. "Dear me," he said, "I shall be late for work, and that will never do." And he got dressed as quickly as he could.' The animal stories, however, tend to be less satisfactory, because they really need pictures to go with them.

Once you've told a few stories of this kind, you may begin to have ideas about getting them published. Your little ones really lapped them up, and if they liked them, other kids would too. Of course, it would help if there were illustrations, but you may feel you have a modicum of talent as an artist, or perhaps your neighbour is really awfully good with her pencil. 'Surely, if I wrote the stories down and did some drawings, or got Maureen-next-door to do some, I could get a book published ...'

Alas, you will usually be disappointed, because the standard required is very high indeed. 'But little Wayne [or little Emma] *loved* the stories,' you protest. The publisher is not impressed. Of course little Wayne loved them, because they're about him and it was you, his Mummy, telling them. But they might not have the

139

same appeal to strangers. As for Maureen's drawings, in an overwhelming majority of cases the illustrations which accompany the submission of an unsolicited book for children are quite incredibly bad. If you don't believe me, ask any publisher.

Now all that is not intended to stop you writing for children if you feel that you want to do so, and if you genuinely like and understand the young. But it is important to realize that it is not the easiest kind of writing, and in fact calls for great skill. Children's books are aimed at the most demanding audience in the world – an audience which has a very low boredom threshold, which is rapidly aware of being talked down to, which likes to be amused but whose sense of humour is not fully developed, which has a limited but expanding vocabulary, which on the whole needs to be able to relate the reading material to its own experience. And all that just refers to the children. You also have in most cases to satisfy the requirements of the adults who buy the books – parents, uncles and aunts, librarians, teachers and booksellers.

Children's Fiction

To write children's stories successfully, you need to follow most of the advice in this book about writing fiction for adults. You must spend just as much time on characterization (after all, children are simple only on the surface – underneath, most of them are as complex as any adult), and you must take just as much care with the dialogue (of which there will perhaps be a higher proportion compared to narrative material than you would have in an adult novel or story). One of the qualities which distinguishes successful children's books from those which do not get serious consideration from publishers is the vitality which carefully drawn characters and vivid dialogue give them.

You must also take great trouble with your choice of words and phrases. If you are writing for young children, remember the value of repetition (seen at its simplest in a nursery rhyme like 'This is the house that Jack built'), but be aware that it has to be carefully handled, keeping the right rhythms, to be effective.

Throughout this book I have placed considerable emphasis on planning, and I should like to suggest that even the shortest of children's books needs to be carefully worked out in advance. It is at this stage, however, that you may have to take a rather simpler approach than you would with adult fiction. Children's books normally have a direct chronological narrative, and the focus of attention is always clearly centred on the child or children whose story it is.

Do make sure, by the way, that problems in the story are solved by the children themselves, and not by adults. For that matter, everything should be told from the child's point of view, rather than the adult's. Geraldine Kaye contrasts two sentences: 'John took up the porridge spoon' and 'John took the porridge spoon in his chubby fist.' The former is unexceptionable, but the latter suggests the indulgent adult looking on, and that is to be avoided. 'Chubby-fistery,' she says, 'is increasingly unacceptable.'

Age Groups

You should have an age group firmly in mind before you start to write a story or a non-fiction piece or book for children. I know of course that children are not all alike – one four-year-old may be much more advanced intellectually than another – but take an average level of intelligence for the age concerned, and then aim specifically at that kind of child, making sure that the length of what you write, its vocabulary and content are all suitable.

The best form of market research that you can do is naturally to talk to children, to read to them if they are too young to read for themselves, and to discover what their likes and dislikes are, for how long at a time it is possible to hold their attention, what balance between the down-to-earth and the imaginative to maintain, and so on. You should also study and analyse books published for children. Talk to teachers, including those who run nursery schools and play-groups – apart from general advice, they may be able to give you specialist guidance on the vocabulary to use for various ages.

The more market research you do, the more clearly you will discover, if you are not aware of it already, that there are vast differences between the various age-groups.

One of the most difficult markets to write for is the teenagers, but if you can get the formula right, you have quite a good chance of success with this type of book. You need to know and sympathize with teenagers; you need to know how they talk and what slang they use (but slang goes out of date very quickly, and you will earn nothing but contempt if your book is full of outmoded expressions – the trick is the very difficult one of capturing the flavour of teenagers' speech without using words which will date it); you need to understand that the greatest sin you can commit in their eyes is to fail to treat them as the intelligent adults they consider themselves to be, so you must never lecture or take up moralizing attitudes, or suggest that your heroes and heroines are immature. Again, study the books which are successfully published for this audience to see how it is done.

The -isms

There has probably never been a period in history when the rights of the individual have been so major an issue. Nowadays we are all aware of the evils of racism, sexism, classism, and even if those who fight most vigorously against such corrupting influences seem sometimes to verge on the hysterical, most people would agree that we should avoid instilling any prejudices into the minds of children. Certainly, publishers, booksellers, librarians, teachers and many other groups are unwilling to support books which have any racist or sexist or classist elements, and your chances of publication will improve if you recognize that we now live in a mixed society and if you write accordingly.

Realism is vital too. Even a fairy story requires its own kind of logic, and while fantasy is acceptable for younger children, they will also appreciate a narrative which reflects their own experiences. The older the age group, the more need for realism there is likely to be, and if you are writing a story with a contemporary setting, remember, for example, that Mum is quite likely to be a working woman, and Dad may well be unemployed. You should also bear in mind the comparative sophistication of quite young children nowadays; television and the fact that parents are not nearly as keen as they used to be on a *'pas devant les enfants'* approach mean that children nowadays know at a very early age a great deal about the realities of life. You may not wish to include any unpleasantness in your writing for children, and you should certainly avoid the kind of realistic dialogue or indeed anything else which might upset parents and teachers, but at the same time you are more likely to succeed with work which acknowledges that all is not perfect in the world, rather than the kind of story which is covered in a smiling veneer. Much as you may deplore it, kids like violence, so you shouldn't shut your eyes to the possibility of including some fairly strong stuff in that direction, though it still seems vital, thank goodness, for the goodies to prevail in the end.

Illustrations

Some writers are also artists. If you are really talented in both fields, you have a chance of becoming very successful. But most writers are not artists. Don't even think of supplying your own illustrations unless you are exceptionally gifted in that direction, and don't, for politeness' sake or for any other reason, allow a friend or relation to illustrate your work unless he is really good. Submit your text as it is, and it will stand a better chance than if accompanied by second-rate pictures. Of course, the converse is also true, and a really talented artist should not allow an incompetent writer to damage his work by giving it an inadequate text. Publishers are quite used to finding artists to illustrate children's books and (though perhaps they are less practised in this instance because it happens more rarely) to finding an author to write a text for existing illustrations. But when text and illustrations are submitted together, and one element is sadly weak, they are sometimes reluctant, unless the other is outstandingly good, to say 'We like the text, but the pictures are dreadful' (or vice versa) and tend simply to reject the whole thing.

If you are intending to submit illustrations for a book you have written, they should of course be of a shape suitable for reproduction in a book. The size is immaterial – large drawings or paintings can be reduced, and miniatures enlarged – but the proportions have to be right, so that the drawings will fit well onto the pages of the book, and it is a good idea for author and artist to agree on the kind of format they have in mind, sticking to one of the sizes of book which publishers most frequently bring out.

Submitting a Children's Book for Publication

The procedure is virtually the same as that explained in Chapter 19. The only important point to make is that it is usual to separate text and pictures, if you should be submitting both. If the book is primarily made up of the text, you can indicate on the typescript where the illustrations are to be placed, though you don't need to leave as much space as they will take up; if the main element in the book is the pictures, then you may pencil the text in, to show exactly where it will go, but it is usual also to provide a typed copy of the words.

You should be aware that many children's books nowadays are written for inclusion in one of a number of popular series, the requirements of which you can discover with a little, fairly simple market research. And don't forget that, as with adult books, it may be easier to get into print with non-fiction (if you can write with sufficient authority) than with fiction.

18

Preparation of the Typescript

The Basic Rules

If you want to sell your work, you will have to type it or have it typed. The days when publishers would consider a manuscript (in the strict sense of the word – i.e. something written in long-hand) are over. A few magazines, including some of the little poetry magazines, will still consider handwritten work, but generally speaking it just has to be typed.

However often the rules are rehearsed at Creative Writing courses, at schools for writers, in Writers' Circles, there are always those who fail to observe the basic instructions for the preparation of a typescript. Like all the rules in this book, the ten which follow are not absolute. Write a brilliant book, and you can ignore half of them and still get published. But for most writers they are worthwhile recommendations. Many of them have to do with the appearance of the typescript, and that really does have an effect on the publisher who is considering it. A well-presented typescript suggests an author with a professional approach and a pride in his work; a messy typescript often comes from a messy, disorganized writer.

So here are the rules – or recommendations, if you prefer:

1. The work should be typed or produced by the printer of a word processor (using 'high-quality' rather than 'draft' mode) in double-spacing (except for poetry and drama (see pp.125–6 and 133–4) and on one side of the paper only. Do not leave spaces between paragraphs unless you intend to indicate a break in the narrative or a total change of subject.

The reason for the double-spacing is that it makes the work easier to read, and also allows room for corrections.

Although a really clean typescript is a pleasure to look at, your work will not be rejected simply because it has a few corrections. Try not to have too many on a page (better to retype a page than make it difficult to read) and make sure that any written corrections are totally legible.

2. Each chapter should begin on a fresh page. Some tutors of Creative Writing insist that the heading and first lines of each chapter should begin half way down the page. I have never found this to be necessary.

3. The paper should be neither smaller than quarto nor bigger than foolscap, and the most acceptable size is A4 (210 x 297 mm). Note, however, that for the American market the preferred size is $11'' \times 8\frac{1}{2}''$.

4. Leave margins at the top and bottom of the paper and on both the left and right sides. The exact measurement of these margins is not of vital importance, but something like 35mm on the left-hand, 25mm at the top and bottom, and 20–25mm on the right-hand side, will not be far wrong.

There are two reasons for this: the margins leave room for corrections, and also for instructions to the printer; and when the printer comes to set the book up in type, he clips the pages onto a kind of stand, and needs space at the edges of the paper so that the clips do not obscure what is written there.

For some reason which I cannot fathom, a great many authors resent having to leave ample margins. Just as they are mean about buying new typewriter ribbons and carbons, so they seem determined to use every square millimetre of paper, as though each sheet cost the earth. It doesn't.

5. It is preferable to use the same typewriter throughout, but if you have to use more than one, try to see that they have the same size of type. In the same way, the size of the margins should not vary from page to page, and each page of the typescript should have the same number of lines except, perhaps, for articles. Be consistent too in such matters as the indentation of paragraphs (five or ten spaces is adequate).

Consistency will make it much easier to calculate the extent, or length of the work. And it also looks better.

6. The pages should be numbered (usually in the top right-hand corner of the paper) from the beginning of the

typescript to the end. Do not number the pages of chapters separately (i.e. beginning at '1' each time).

7. The first page of the typescript should show the title of the work and the author's name or pseudonym, and should also carry his name and address (or the name and address of his agent). It is also helpful to indicate on this page the approximate number of words in the typescript.

It is not necessary to count every single word in your typescript, nor is it helpful to give an exact figure, because the publisher, strangely enough, wants the number of words to include also the spaces at the end of paragraphs and chapters. The way to calculate the wordage of a full-length book is as follows:

Count 50 full-length lines and find the average number of words to a line – e.g. 50 lines giving a total of 560 words means an average of 11.2 words per line.

Average the number of lines over 10 typical pages – e.g. 10 pages giving a total of 245 lines means an average of 24.5 lines per page. (But please note that you should try to have the same number of lines on every page.)

Multiply the average number of words to a line by the average number of lines to a page; this will give you the average number of words to a page – e.g. $11.2 \times 24.5 = 274$.

Multiply the average number of words per page by the number of pages in the typescript (counting short pages at the beginnings and ends of chapters as full pages). Round off the figure to the nearest thousand (or the nearest five thousand).

If you are trying to establish the word count of an article or short story, you can find out the average number of words per line, as explained above, and then multiply that figure by the actual number of lines in the piece. Round the figure off to the nearest hundred, or even the nearest fifty.

8. If you are submitting your work to a British newspaper or magazine, add the words 'First British Serial Rights' or the initials 'FBSR' on the title page of your typescript (see also Chapter 14). But you do not do so if you are sending it to a book publisher.

When you sell an article or a short story or a poem to a

newspaper or magazine, you do not sell, or even lease, your copyright in the work, and all you grant, in return for appropriate payment, is the right to publish the piece once, prior to its appearance anywhere in book form. This is known as 'First British Serial Rights'. You do not give the newspaper or magazine the right to publish the piece in hardcovers or paperback or to negotiate bookclub sales, or sell foreign rights – or even to allow it to appear in another newspaper or magazine at a later date (known as Second Serial Rights; incidentally, 'Second' means 'second and subsequent' – one does not refer to Third or Fourth Serial Rights). If you submit a book to a publisher, however, he will expect to control some or all of those rights, and what you will offer to him, or at least what he will expect to buy, will be Volume Rights (i.e. the right to produce the work in book form, plus, in some cases, various subsidiary rights – for further details, see my book *An Author's Guide to Publishing*).

9. You should type your name and address again on the last page of the typescript. It is also helpful to put 'The End' after the last line of the text.

Although it is not common nowadays to include 'The End' in the printed copy, and indeed you may not wish it to appear, having it on the last page of the typescript does make it clear that there is no more to come (which is not always self-evident.).

10. One of the most vexed questions is how to fasten together your completed typescript. My own preference when I was a publisher was for no fastening at all. I liked the typescript to consist of separate sheets (properly numbered, of course, in case I dropped them all onto the floor and had to sort them out again) and kept tidy in one of those boxes that typing paper comes in. My pet aversion was paperclips, which have an unpleasant habit of picking up other papers from a busy editor's desk. I did not object to chapters or batches of pages being secured with a staple, provided that there was only one, in the top left-hand corner.

All publishers seem to differ in their likes and dislikes in this matter, but I think they all agree in loathing the kind of typescript which has been fastened together in one great solid lump. It is extremely heavy and awkward to read.

Christopher Derrick, in his entertaining and instructive book *Reader's Report*, writes of one other method of presenting a typescript:

> From time to time one comes across an author who has decided to ... give the publisher's reader a real treat. His typescript arrives in book form, properly bound, and it's a joy to behold. He has chosen a pure hand-made rag paper of dazzling whiteness, and he's used one of those fancy typewriters that have proportionate spacing and a carbon-paper ribbon, so that the novel appears to have been printed already, and in a luxury format. Each page has been laid out beautifully; and the whole thing has been bound up in purple puma-skin and the heaviest of boards, with headbands and gilt edges and marbled endpapers and a lovely broad silk marker. The title and the proud father's name are tooled in gold upon the spine. You gasp with admiration when you see this miracle of craftsmanship.
>
> But efforts of this kind are always wasted, and for two reasons. In the first place, compositors always prefer to work from single sheets; and if this novel were to be accepted, it would have to be ripped to shreds almost at once. The thought is enough to break anyone's heart. But it won't be accepted. By every literary standard and for every practical purpose of publishing, *books submitted in this kind of format are always worthless*. Nobody knows why this should be so: it amounts to a law of nature, mysterious but absolute. Don't suppose that your novel will be an exception.

Copyright

Many writers put a copyright notice on the first page of the typescript (in the form 'Copyright © John Smith 1986'). Such a notice has to be printed in published books, but it is not necessary on a typescript. You are already protected.

Any original work which you write is your copyright, from the moment when you set the words down on paper, and no one else can copy it, or print it, without your permission. Even the letters that you write to friends are your copyright – the person who receives the letter owns it as a physical entity, but you still retain ownership of the writing in it. Copyright normally exists during the lifetime of the author and for seventy years after his death.

You should never part with your copyright, unless under very exceptional circumstances, and if a publisher asks you to do so, you should take advice from a body such as the Society of Authors, or from a solicitor, or at very least from an experienced writer (if you have an agent he will, of course, deal with the matter for you). What you do normally is *license* a publisher to produce your work. The licence will detail which rights in your work (e.g. paperback rights, book club rights) are granted to the publisher, and which remain in your control. The licence may last for the entire term of copyright, but there are usually clauses which allow for the cancellation of the licence if the book goes out of print, or if the publisher fails to adhere to the terms of the contract.

Copyright works both ways: no one can steal your work, but equally you cannot use other authors' words without permission, which usually involves the payment of a fee, unless the extract is very short. Some authors feel that they can overcome any problems in this direction by paraphrasing any work that they want to quote, but there are dangers here because you may be accused of plagiarism (purloining the ideas of others). For practical purposes, however, you need not worry too much about obtaining permission until you reach a stage when your work is actually going to be published, and your publisher will then be able to advise and help you with this problem.

In general terms, there is no copyright in ideas. Many authors worry that publishers who reject their work will pinch their ideas and pass them on to other writers. If this ever occurs, it is likely to be by accident rather than design.

Equally, there is no copyright in titles. On the other hand you should avoid giving your book an already well-known title, because you could be accused of 'passing off', which roughly means trying to persuade people to buy your book in the mistaken belief that it is the famous one.

19

Selling Your Work

Getting into Print

Just as there are no rules about writing, so there are none about how to get into print, but if you want to be published, you might consider carefully the following points:

Whatever you write, you need to be totally sincere about it. Writers who set out deliberately to produce a bestseller rarely succeed unless they believe totally in what they are writing. And if you think it doesn't apply to the 'formula' style of writing (e.g. romantic fiction), just see how far you get with your tongue in your cheek!

Don't write without authority. Get your facts right, do your research properly, and don't expect to publish a non-fiction book unless you really are an expert (and preferably have a reputation in that field too).

Be original if you can. It is worth trying to keep an eye on trends, but remember that there will be a considerable gap between the books which are currently setting any particular trend, and the publication of your own, as yet unwritten, book – a gap of two years as a minimum, allowing a year for writing and at least a year for finding a publisher and the completion of the publishing process. If you are not yourself a trend-setter, then you probably need to be a crystal-gazer to know what sort of books are going to be in fashion in two or three years' time.

Be patient (remember how many successful books have started out as failures), persevere and don't build your hopes too high.

Accept the fact that no publisher has an obligation to publish your book. Your job is to make him want to. Get the beginning right (because you must hook him, and the eventual reader, right from the start), and don't let the standard drop.

Finding a Market

I must make it clear that this chapter is chiefly concerned with full-length fiction. Some information about selling other forms of writing is given in Chapters 11 to 17.

Once your work is neatly typed, you are ready to send it off to a publisher. But which one? You can of course open *The Writers' and Artists' Yearbook* to an appropriate section and stick a pin in. But you may be wasting your time by sending your material to the wrong place.

Visit bookshops and libraries and try to find out by looking at the books on the shelves which publishers bring out the kind of book that you have written. Ask the bookseller or the librarian for advice. And you can write to publishers for their catalogues, from which you will be able to see not only what sort of books they publish but what will be appearing under their imprint in the next six months or so.

Don't expect to do this market research quickly – it is something which takes time, for you want not only to be sure that the publisher you choose is likely to be interested in the type of book you have written, and that its length will be acceptable, but also that within the particular genre you have not offended against any taboos.

How would you know about various publishers' taboos? By reading the books that they publish. If, for instance, you have written a romantic novel but have indulged in a fairly torrid bedroom scene, you will want to send it to a publisher of romantic novels who is prepared to accept more than a hint of explicit sex.

Submitting Your Work to a Publisher

When you have decided where to submit your book, you can simply parcel it up and send it off. You will do better, however, to write to the publisher first, asking if you may submit it. Before you do so, telephone and ask the switchboard operator for the name of the editorial director, so that you can address your letter to him personally.

Don't write a crawling letter ('I would be greatly honoured if such a distinguished publishing company as yours were to take on my humble work') or a jokey letter ('my Mum thinks it's ever so good, but it is just possible that she's a little biased') or an aggressive letter ('I wish you to publish this book. Kindly state your terms by return'). Instead, write simply and briefly – the editor does not want to wade through ten pages of detailed synopsis – giving a description of your book in a few lines. 'May I please send for your consideration the novel which I have written? It concerns the adventures of Richard Lionheart during the Crusades and is approximately 80,000 words in length.' That will give the publisher enough to go on at this stage.

Don't tell the publisher how much your friends have enjoyed your work. Since he does not know your friends, he will not be prepared to accept their opinion, and in any case he will suspect that they would not have told you the truth. On the other hand, if someone famous, especially someone in the literary world, has read your book and is prepared to endorse it, that is worth mentioning.

Enclose a stamped, addressed envelope for the reply.

If the response is favourable, you can mail your material to the publisher. Enclose postage for its return if he does not want to add it to his list. If you don't trust the mails and can go to the publisher's office, you can leave your parcel with the receptionist, but don't expect to see an editor, and never ask to see anyone so that you can explain something about the book. It should be its own ambassador, and if you have to explain it, you haven't done your work properly.

Many writers who have tried in vain to find a publisher begin to believe that none of them is ever interested in a first novel. It is not true. It may be much more difficult to get started nowadays, but hundreds of first novels are still published every year, and there are dozens of publishers, including most of the paperback houses, which are constantly on the look-out for new fiction writers.

Synopsis and Specimen Chapter

Some publishers will agree to consider a synopsis and a specimen chapter or chapters, and it is fairly common for non-fiction books to be commissioned on this basis. In my publishing days, however, I never commissioned a novel on the basis of a synopsis and specimen pages, except from an author who was already established on my list. In most cases, the beginner just has to sit down and write the whole thing to be sure of getting full consideration.

I have seen it suggested that, after finishing a book, an author should send a publisher a synopsis and a few specimen pages extracted more or less at random from the typescript, rather than submitting the complete book. It seems to me an appalling idea. It may save postage, but I doubt if any publisher would welcome it or be able to make any kind of sensible judgement from so little material.

Waiting for a Verdict

Regrettably from the author's point of view, a great many publishers take a very long time to consider a book. That there are frequently good reasons for the delay is little consolation when you are waiting for a verdict. How long should you wait? I would suggest that you cannot expect to hear in less than four weeks. If you have had no response three months after you submitted the book, you should write a polite letter asking for news of it. If six months go by, it is time to start being stroppy and demanding the return of your typescript. If nothing results from that, maybe you should consult a solicitor.

If your book is rejected, don't expect to be told why. It may seem very unhelpful, but most publishers have enough trouble in coping with the books that they *are* going to publish, and do not have time to involve themselves in possibly lengthy correspondence about books which they are *not* going to publish.

You must never be discouraged by a rejection. Try another publisher. Remember that John Braine had to send

Room at the Top to thirty-eight publishers before it was accepted, and Christianna Brand's first detective story was turned down by nineteen publishers before the Bodley Head took it and launched her on a successful career – and there are many other similar stories. You need to persevere. And if you receive a letter which, despite rejecting your material, includes some remarks sounding like an expression of interest in you as an author or of regard for your work, be greatly heartened – publishers don't make a habit of writing such letters unless they really mean it. On the other hand, if you get a whole series of rejections, without any word of the slightest encouragement, perhaps you should stop and ask yourself whether the book is really as good as you think it is.

Agents

Many new authors believe that their only chance of getting a book accepted is if they can find an agent to represent them. This is not true. You may have heard that the typescripts which arrive direct from authors are known to publishers as 'the slush pile'. It sounds a very derogatory term, but full attention is paid to the books in it, and indeed many publishers prefer to take books from the slush pile than through agents, because they will have greater control over the subsidiary rights and because the terms of the contract may be less generous to the author.

On the other hand, it is certainly true that publishers pay particular attention to books which come to them from agents, because they know that the books have already been through the sifting net and must have some qualities which the agent believes to be saleable, and also because, if the agent knows his business, he will send the books to the publishers who are most likely to be interested in them.

So, yes, it is good to have an agent. But it is far more difficult to find an agent who will take you on, if you are an unpublished author, than it is to find a publisher. This is partly because there are far fewer agents than publishers, but also because the agent has to make his living from the commissions he takes – normally ten per cent (which reminds me of the story of the famous

Writing for Pleasure and Profit

author who asked to be cremated and for ten per cent of his ashes to be scattered over his agent) – and will not take on new authors unless he is reasonably certain that they are going to earn a fairly good annual income from their writing, the commission from which will pay his costs and give him some profit.

Agents can be extremely helpful. They know the market-place better than any author can, they send your book out at their own expense, they negotiate contracts, and they act as a buffer between author and publisher in the case of disagreement, often arguing more forcefully on the author's behalf than he could himself. They will also usually secure better terms from a publisher than the author is likely to be able to achieve by himself, and they may sometimes be more successful than the publisher (but by no means always) in the sale of subsidiary rights.

Do not be misled by that last sentence into thinking that if you have an agent you will become very much richer than if you deal directly with a publisher. An agent-negotiated contract is often significantly better for the author, but it does not necessarily mean making a fortune rather than receiving only a pittance. If your book is accepted by a reputable publisher, he will not set out to cheat you. What he pays you may seem a ridiculously small amount, but if you check it out, you will probably find that it is pretty much the going rate for the kind of book you have written. The publisher is in a buyer's market, and if you don't like the terms he offers and refuse to let him publish your book he will probably shrug his shoulders – there are plenty of fish in the sea. However, if it became known that, in comparison with other publishers, he was habitually under-paying his authors, that might cause his nets to catch far fewer fish, and for that reason he will not usually risk treating his authors unfairly. An agent will see that he doesn't, but you needn't be too worried if you are not represented, and indeed, it may be better for many first-time writers to submit their books direct to publishers rather than to waste their time in trying to find an agent, which, as I have already pointed out, may be difficult.

If you still want an agent, you may stand a better chance if you apply to the newer, smaller firms, which are more likely to have room on their lists of clients.

Vanity Publishing

Most would-be writers who have been to Creative Writing classes, or who have studied *The Writers' and Artists' Yearbook*, will have been warned against Vanity Publishing, but what exactly is meant by the term?

If Mr X, who cannot get anyone to publish his poetry, pays a local printer to produce a slim volume and then gives or sells copies to his friends, you may think him vain, but it is not vanity publishing in the technical sense as the term is used within the book trade. Nor would it be if some well-known publisher were to write his memoirs and have them published by his own firm (since he would not personally pay for the publication of his book and indeed would expect to receive royalties on sales in the normal way). It is not even vanity publishing, though nearer the mark, when an author persuades a regular trade publisher to take on a book by paying a share of the costs or perhaps guaranteeing to buy a substantial number of copies (the point being that in such cases the publisher does not cheat the author, who may well get his money back).

Those examples do not involve any deception of the author. Vanity publishing usually does.

The normal arrangement is for the author to pay the vanity publisher a large sum of money (several thousand pounds), which is supposedly his *share* of production and other costs, but which in most cases covers all costs and the publisher's profits. The publisher commits himself to having copies of the book (usually about 400) available prior to publication for purposes of publicity, review, promotion and sales, and promises to pay the author a royalty of 33 1/3 per cent on all sales. This, as the vanity publisher is at great pains to point out, is a substantially higher royalty than an author is likely to receive from a regular trade publisher.

However, although in conversation with the author (but never in the contract) the publisher may speak of major sales efforts and of the facilities he enjoys for national distribution of the book, there is little likelihood of any sales, apart from the copies sold to the author, who, though entitled to purchase them at a high discount, will not receive any royalties on such sales. The vanity publisher will probably not have printed more than the 400 or so copies referred to above.

The activities of vanity publishers are not illegal, and I suppose there may be some around who are honest and fair in all their dealings. But in conversation and sometimes in correspondence a vanity publisher is likely to mislead the authors who come to him in a number of ways: he may suggest that he will perform satisfactorily all sorts of standard publishing functions which he has no intention of even attempting; he may give the impression that the author is merely contributing to the costs of producing the book, whereas he is in fact paying for all of it; and the author will go away believing that he stands every chance of getting his money back very quickly, but vanity publishers rarely, if ever, pay out money – they only take it in. Their contracts, however, make no promises to do anything which they fail to do, and while almost every clause of these documents is so worded that no sensible author should dream of signing it, once it is signed, there is no redress.

You can usually recognize vanity publishers because at an early stage it will become plain that they expect you to contribute to the costs of production. Earlier still you may pick out their Press advertisements asking for the submission of typescripts. Ordinary publishers do not advertise in that way. If you are ever tempted to go to a vanity publisher, don't. Assuming that you have failed to interest a regular publisher in your book, and have the money to get it into print yourself, go to a printer and ask him to give you a price for producing however many copies you want. It will be a lot less costly than the deal that you would get from a vanity publisher, and you will get all the money back on any copies that you sell. You may indeed sell quite a large number of copies if you have the time and energy to visit bookshops up and down the country, persuading them to stock your book.

Acceptance

Oh, the joy if your book is accepted for publication! I have written at length in *An Author's Guide to Publishing* of all that is likely to happen, or not to happen, to your book and of the pleasures and pitfalls awaiting a published author. Here I will confine myself to one suggestion, and that is to take advice about the publishing contract that you will be sent for signature. But don't ask your usual solicitor. It's not that I have anything against him – he may be an absolute wiz at drawing up wills and conveyancing – but unless he is also an expert on authors' contracts, which is fairly unlikely, he may be out of his depth. The unusual nature of publishing is reflected in the complexity of publishers' agreements, and you really need to know your way around them before giving an author advice.

If you do not have an agent, the best thing you can do is to join the Society of Authors (see p. 166). At the very least, take your contract to your Writers' Circle and ask the advice of anyone in it who has already been published. And don't be afraid to ask your publisher to make changes in it. If he has got as far as drawing up a contract, he won't be put off your book because you ask him to improve the terms. And he can always say 'no'.

Bestsellers

As a sort of postscript to this chapter, let me add a little list of the particular qualities which may make a bestselling novel, though the degree to which they are present may vary considerably.

Originality. Perhaps this is the least essential ingredient.

Conflict. Reader Identification. Suspense. These are the three prime requirements of a good story – plenty of action, a sympathetic principal character and the kind of narrative which hooks the reader on the very first page and keeps him reading right to the end, because he wants to know what happens next.

Credibility. This is very much a demand of our age. Readers are willing to suspend their disbelief, but never too far, and the author must carry conviction in telling his story.

Topicality. I do not mean by this that the story is inspired by some nine-days'-wonder reported in the newspapers, or even that the book has been written to coincide with some forthcoming anniversary of a major event, but that it should appear at just the right moment to catch the popular taste. Many great bestsellers have somehow sensed emotions buried, or perhaps partially hidden, in the public's consciousness, which have been ready to surface just as the book has appeared.

A good title. What makes a good title is hard to define. I always like the story of Sir Stanley Unwin trying to persuade the book trade that he had a bestseller on his hands. 'The title is hopeless,' they all told him. '*Expedition* has such an old-fashioned ring to it, and as for the word in front of it, no one will be able to remember it, or pronounce it if they do.' The book was, of course, *The Kon-Tiki Expedition*.

20

The Rewards of Writing

Payment for Your Work

It is impossible to give any guidance as to the rewards you may expect from the publication of a book, whether it is fiction or non-fiction. It can vary from almost nothing to a fortune. Equally, there are no standard figures for royalties (often set on a sliding scale, which means that the author is paid at a higher rate after a given number of copies has been sold), which are normally expressed as a percentage of the published price for sales in the British home market and often a lesser percentage, or a percentage based on the price received by the publisher, on export sales.

The remarks in that paragraph must seem extremely vague, but books vary so much in every way that one cannot be more helpful. If you are offered an advance, or royalties, which seem to you on the low side, seek advice about your particular case from those with experience, or ask your publisher to explain why the offer is in those specific terms. The only other useful thing that I can say is that the less you expect, the less likely you are to be disappointed.

Word for word, you can probably make far more in proportion if you manage to sell a short story or an article to a magazine or newspaper. Payment for publication in these outlets is comparatively good, based on the number of words you write. It is fairly common practice with local newspapers for no payment to be made until you submit an invoice, which you should do immediately following the publication of your work. Even as a beginner, if you press for it, you may receive payment at the full union rate; on the other hand, as is to be expected, an editor will normally offer less to a newcomer. While it may be reasonable to accept a low payment for the first two or three items you sell him, you could then go to see him and try to negotiate something better. He will probably be fairly easily persuaded into increasing the fees if you can provide him regularly with good and interesting material.

The rewards for the publication of poetry are likely to be very poor. Often they will be non-existent, the argument being that sales are so small as not to justify the payment of any royalties to the poet, and moreover that the mere fact of publication enhances his reputation; when that reputation has been solidly established, he will be able to command a good fee – a fine example of jam tomorrow. Nowadays the reading of poetry, sometimes in pubs, has become popular, and many contemporary poets add to their incomes by the fees they receive on such occasions, and by the sale of copies of their work (sometimes self-duplicated) to those who have heard their performance.

Work which is accepted by the BBC is paid for at fixed rates, based on the length of the transmission, both for radio and for television. Whether you receive the maximum or the minimum fee, or something in between, depends on your fame and the regularity with which you write for the Corporation. Fees obtained from ITV are likely to be higher than those paid by the BBC.

Remuneration for stage plays is derived only to a comparatively small extent from sales of the printed copies. The major portion should come from performance fees, both professional and amateur.

PLR

Public Lending Right, under which moneys were first paid to authors, after long campaigning, in 1984, is a system of rewarding them for the borrowing of their books from public libraries in the United Kingdom. Whereas previously the author received only the royalty due to him on the purchase by the library of the copy or copies of his book, and nothing additional, however often the book was read, now a minuscule payment per borrowing is made, provided that the book meets certain requirements and is borrowed a minimum number of times. The funds from which the payments are made, provided by the Government, are inevitably insufficient, but anything is better than nothing, and authors must simply hope that in the course of time the scheme will be extended and more adequately financed. Meanwhile, all authors who succeed in getting a book published should register for PLR. Full details may be obtained from the Registrar, Public Lending Right Office, Bayheath House, Prince Regent Street, Stockton-on-Tees, Cleveland TS18 1DF.

Prizes

Many prizes are given annually to books. The most famous and prestigious of the British awards is the Booker Prize, which goes to a novel of high literary merit and is usually won by an established author. But you don't necessarily have to be famous or a highbrow writer to win a literary prize. There is, for instance, the Betty Trask Award, the terms of which specify that the author who wins it shall not have been published previously and that the book must be a novel of a non-experimental nature. Both the Booker and the Betty Trask are for full-length works of fiction, but there are dozens of others prizes for all kinds of books – indeed, *The Writers' and Artists' Yearbook* has more than twenty pages listing them all.

The effect of prizes on book sales varies. But even in those cases where few extra copies are sold, the prestige is bound to assist the author's career as a writer, and there is usually some financial reward.

In addition to the annual awards, many publishers, newspapers, literary and other organizations run competitions from time to time, and if you keep your eyes open you will find that, whether you write novels, short stories, non-fiction, children's books, poetry or drama, there is almost always, at any time of the year, a competition for your kind of writing taking place somewhere in the British Isles. The financial rewards may not be very great, but publication is often guaranteed for the winner and the encouragement to be gained from winning is enormous.

Writers' Circles

Writing is a lonely business. Writers often say that as though it set their trade apart from all other occupations. Many creative activities are equally lonely, and so too are a large number of hobbies. One might well say that stamp-collecting is a lonely business.

However, whether or not it is worthy of special mention, writing certainly *is* lonely, and it is also, as I said at the beginning of this book, difficult both to teach and, without guidance, to learn. Out of those two facts has come the establishment of a large number of Writers' Circles or Clubs or Associations. I am not referring here to national organizations such as the Society of Authors and the Writers' Guild of Great Britain, which exist to represent authors who in effect are professional or at least established to the extent, precarious in some cases, of having been published. Writers' Circles, on the other hand, are local, being set up in cities and towns, and though many successful authors belong to them, their main membership consists of those who are merely aspiring to be published.

Most Writers' Circles meet regularly once or twice a month (sometimes weekly), and they usually offer criticism and advice. The normal arrangement is that members take their work to a meeting and read it out, and the remainder of those present make any comments which occur to them; this can be extremely helpful not only because of receiving advice about one's own work but because one is expected to comment on other members' writing, which develops the critical faculties.

Perhaps the greatest pleasure and value to be gained by joining a Writers' Circle, however, is the companionship. The loneliness of writing is not simply something which is evident when the author is actually at work. It also comes from the fact that often the writer has no one who really understands his interest and problems. Meeting other authors is usually a joy, simply because they are all on the same wavelength.

A list of Writers' Circles, compiled by Jill Dick, can be obtained at a modest price from Laurence Pollinger Ltd, 18 Maddox Street, London W1R 0EU.

Out of the Writers' Circles have come the schools for writers, the majority of which run for a weekend. The Writers' Summer School, the oldest and most prestigious of these institutions, takes place at Swanwick in Derbyshire every year and lasts for a whole week. Details can be obtained from the Secretary: Brenda Courtie, The New Vicarage, Parson Street, Woodford Halse, Daventry, Northants NN11 3RE.

There are also many classes in Creative Writing organized by local Further Education authorities, and courses are also available at the Arvon Foundation and at many privately run centres throughout the country.

Collaboration

If you join a Writers' Circle, you will undoubtedly make friends. Perhaps you will even find so kindred a spirit that the two of you decide that you could work together.

Some of those who want to write say that they are full of ideas but either haven't the time or haven't the ability to make anything of them, while others are only too ready and able to write if only they could think what to write about. The answer might be collaboration.

It doesn't have to work on a strict division of the labour as suggested in the previous paragraph. Some collaborations begin simply because both the writers concerned share the same interest and discover perhaps that each is intending to write on that subject; working together, they pool their knowledge and take equal responsibility for any necessary research; ideas may come from both partners, and often both will share the actual writing; with luck the result is a better book than either would have produced on his own.

Some partnerships have even succeeded in producing novels by taking it in turns to write the chapters, but if you are going to do that, you probably need a particularly close rapport with your collaborator and the ability of both to write in the same style.

Collaboration does not depend on both partners being writers. It maybe that one of the pair will have expert knowledge but no writing ability, while the other, though interested in the subject, cannot claim a deep knowledge of it but is a practising writer.

Like all writing, collaboration demands a certain amount of experiment, in this case to find which method suits the partnership best.

Organizations for Writers

There are two national organizations for writers:

The Society of Authors, established in 1884, is a registered trade union but is not affiliated to the TUC. Its address is: 84 Drayton Gardens, London SW10 9SB.

The Writers' Guild of Great Britain is a registered trade union affiliated to the TUC. Its address is; 430 Edgware Road, London W2 1EH.

It is my firm belief that any writer who achieves publication should join one or other of these societies. Many authors baulk at doing so, because the subscriptions are not cheap. So why should you join?

Firstly, members receive many benefits, including not only such predictable entitlements as magazines and the opportunity of attending various literary events but also advice on contracts and many other matters of business import to a writer, including in some circumstances legal action on his behalf.

Secondly, and perhaps more importantly, these two organizations, frequently working together, are the only bodies which can speak with any authority and power on behalf of authors to publishers, to broadcasting and television companies, to the government. The individual author is permanently in a buyer's market, unless and until he reaches bestseller status, and is always at the mercy of those who buy his work. On the whole, publishers are not going to cheat you, but they may sometimes treat you less fairly than they should, which is why you should not sign a contract, unless you are very sure of yourself, without taking advice. But individual contracts are not really the point, which is that, although the Publishers Association does not lay down any terms that all its members should follow, publishers all tend to stick roughly to the same kind of contracts, which from the author's point of view could in many respects be more generous. An agent often gets better terms for his clients, but even the largest of agents cannot speak for as many authors as the Society of Authors and The Writers' Guild, and the more writers who join them, the more effectively can they make their voice heard.

Thirdly, I think authors should join with the thought that at least a part of their annual subscription is a kind of thanksgiving for what the Society and the Guild have achieved in the past. Few authors are well paid. The majority cannot afford to live solely by writing but require either a private income or a job which allows them a little free time for authorship. But if there has been any improvement in the author's lot over the past hundred years, it is largely due to the Society of Authors and, more recently, to the Society working in co-operation with the Writers' Guild.

A Final Word

'Writing,' according to Georges Simenon, 'is not a profession but a vocation of unhappiness.' He also said, 'I think everyone who does not *need* to be a writer, who thinks he can do something else, ought to do something else.' For my part, I'd leave Monsieur Simenon to his sour gloom. I think writing is one of the most enjoyable pursuits imaginable – even if you are dependent on it for your living, and even if the money doesn't come in, and even if you are never satisfied with what you write. You may think that it's all very well for me, as a published writer, to say that. But I honestly don't think that being published is the be-all and end-all of writing. I have written a great deal that hasn't been published, but have still derived much pleasure from it – from the joy of creativity and the satisfaction of completing a job to the best of my ability. Another reason why writing is so enjoyable is that you can never finish learning about it – it is inexhaustible.

In this book I have tried to share with you some of the things that I have learnt as an editor and an author and a teacher. I hope they may be of some help. But remember that they are not the last word. There is no last word.

There are no rules.

Books to Help You

In recent years large numbers of guides and manuals for would-be writers have appeared, including the *Writer's Guide* series published by Allison & Busby, *The Way to Write* series published by Elm Tree Books, and the *Writing ...* series published by A. & C. Black. Other publishers, notably Robert Hale, have also entered the field. Almost all such books currently on the market can be recommended, but in the list which follows I have selected those which seem to me to deal with their subjects in the most helpful way.

Please note that many of the books on this list are revised from time to time, so it is always worth making sure that you have the latest edition. Other books have been included despite the fact that they are out of print, but it should still be possible to obtain them from libraries.

Basic Requirements

A good dictionary. It is really worth getting something at least as comprehensive as *The Shorter Oxford English Dictionary* (Oxford University Press).

A thesaurus. I am never quite sure of the value of a thesaurus – neither of mine normally seems to supply the word I am really looking for, and once I open *Roget's Thesaurus* (Longmans) or the much more helpfully arranged *New Collins Thesaurus* (Collins) I tend to waste a lot of time in just reading it. However, many writers consider a thesaurus indispensable.

Books about Words and Language

A Dictionary of Modern English Usage by H.W. Fowler (Second edition revised by Sir Ernest Gowers, Oxford Paperbacks). The fascinating book which is normally known as *Fowler's Modern English Usage*.

Usage and Abusage by Eric Partridge (Penguin).

The Penguin Dictionary of Historical Slang by Eric Partridge (abridged by Jacqueline Simpson, Penguin).

Hart's Rules for Compositors and Readers at the University Press Oxford (Oxford University Press). A useful little book which gives advice on such matters as when to put full stops after abbreviations, and when not to, the plurals of words ending in -o, hyphened and non-hyphened words, etc.

The Oxford Dictionary for Writers and Editors (Oxford University Press). Much like *Hart's Rules*, but arranged in conventional dictionary style rather than by subject.

The Elements of Style by William Strunk Jr and E.B. White (Collier-Macmillan). Don't be put off by the book's American origin. It's a good little manual.

The Nuts and Bolts of Writing by Michael Legat (Hale). A book written at my publisher's request in the hope that it would help to raise the standard of spelling, punctuation and grammar in the typescripts submitted to his firm.

Good English by G.H. Vallins (Pan Books).

General Books about Writing

Becoming a Writer by Dorothea Brande (Papermac). Although it is well over sixty years old, this is the best book on the subject I have ever read.

From Pen to Paper by Pamela Frankau (Heinemann). An entertaining account of her writing life.

Approaches to Writing by Paul Horgan (Bodley Head). Useful advice from a fine American author.

The Making of a Novelist by Margaret Thomson Davis (Allison & Busby). Although this is primarily an autobiography, it contains much information on the making of a novel.

Reader's Report by Christopher Derrick (Gollancz). A publisher's reader writes about his job, and that of the author.

Writing Step by Step by Jean Saunders (Allison & Busby). A good book for beginners.

Teach Yourself Creative Writing by Dianne Doubtfire (Hodder & Stoughton).

Books on Specific Forms of Writing

Writing a Novel by John Braine (Eyre Methuen).

The Craft of Novel-Writing by Dianne Doubtfire (Allison & Busby)

Plotting the Novel by Michael Legat (Hale).

Aspects of the Novel by E.M. Forster (Penguin).

Writing Popular Fiction by Rona Randall (Black).

Writing Crime Fiction by H.R.F. Keating (Black).

The Craft of Writing Romance by Jean Saunders (Allison & Busby).

How to Write Historical Novels by Michael Legat (Allison & Busby).

The Way to Write Science Fiction by Brian Stableford (Elm Tree).

How to Write Short Stories for Magazines by Donna Baker (Allison & Busby).

Non-Fiction Books: A Writer's Guide by Michael Legat (Hale).

The Successful Author's Handbook by Gordon Wells (Papermac).

How to Write for Children by Tessa Krailing (Allison & Busby).

How to Write for Teenagers by David Silwyn Williams (Allison & Busby).

Freelance Writing for Newspapers by Jill Dick (Black).

The Way to Write Magazine Articles by John Hines (Elm Tree).

The Magazine Writer's Handbook by Gordon Wells (Allison & Busby).

Writing for Radio by Rosemary Horstmann (Black).

The Way to Write for Television by Eric Paice (Elm Tree).
Writing for the BBC, the BBC's own handbook, published by them.
The Craft of Writing Poetry by Alison Chisholm (Allison & Busby).
Becoming a Playwright by David Campton (Hale).
Writing about Travel by Morag Campbell (Black).

Books about Publishing

The Truth about Publishing by Stanley Unwin (Allen & Unwin). The publishing process explained in detail.
An Author's Guide to Publishing by Michael Legat (Hale). An author-friendly manual giving comprehensive coverage of all aspects of the author/publisher relationship.
Dear Author ... by Michael Legat (Allison & Busby). Letters from a publisher to authors prospective and practised.
Understanding Publishers' Contracts by Michael Legat (Hale). What the clauses of your contract mean, what it should contain, what points you should not accept.

Books on Getting Published

Writers' and Artists' Yearbook (Black). Published annually. Lists of markets for books, magazines, plays, radio, TV, painting, photography, music, agents, etc, plus general information.
The Writers' Handbook, edited by Barry Turner (Macmillan/PEN). Published annually. Similar to the *Writers' and Artists' Yearbook*, but concentrates on markets for writing, and adds informative and often entertaining comments on the firms it lists.
Writer's Market, (Writer's Digest Books). Published annually. Full details of the American markets.
Publishing Your Own Book by Jon Wynne-Tyson (Centaur Press). This is little more than a pamphlet, but it contains just about all the information that a self-publishing author needs.

How to Publish Your Poetry by Peter Finch (Allison & Busby). A comprehensive guide to the specialist needs of the poet.

Miscellaneous

Research for Writers by Ann Hoffmann (A. & C. Black). The standard work on the subject.

Book Indexing by M.D. Anderson (Cambridge University Press). A brief but helpful guide.

The Guinness Book of Names by Leslie Dunkling (Guinness Books). An invaluable and immensely entertaining reference book.

Historical Costumes of England by Nancy Bradfield (Harrap). This is one of the best of the many books available.

A book of quotations. I like *The Oxford Dictionary of Quotations* (Oxford University Press).

The Directory of Writers' Circles compiled by Jill Dick (Laurence Pollinger). A regularly updated list of writers' groups in Britain.

Index

Index 175

Putting the reader wise, 85–6
Pygmalion, 42

Qualities needed by a writer, 16–20
Quotation marks, 91
Quiller-Couch, Arthur, 59
Quintillian, Marcus, 57

Radio, 135–7, 162
Radio drama, 136–7
Raine, Kathleen, 125
Rayner, Claire, 25–6, 100
Reade, Charles, 68
Reader identification, 78–80, 159
Reader's Digest, 24
Reader's Report, 39, 148–9
Reading, 20–1
Reading aloud, 45, 49, 55, 57–8, 86, 128
Reading, recommended, 169–72
Repetitions, 43–4, 60
Research, 59, 94–7, 105–6, 114
Revision, 56–62, 99, 124–5
Rhythm, 49, 58, 121–4
Rodgers, Richard, 41
Room at the Top, 155

Second serial rights, 118, 148
Secret Life of Walter Mitty, The, 75
Selling your work, 101–2, 111–13, 118–19, 125–6, 133, 144, 147–8, 151–60, 161–2
Sentences, 35, 48, 54–5
Settings, 92–3
Shakespeare, William, 39
Shaw, Bernard, 42
Short stories, 26–7, 98–103
Silk Maker, The, 92
Silverlight, John, 39
Simenon, Georges, 167
Simplicity, 49, 58, 116
Slang, 44–5, 129
Society of Authors, The, 159, 164, 166–7
Spelling, 46–7
Spillane, Mickey, 25, 26
Sprig of Broom, The, 39, 43
Stevenson, Robert Louis, 92
Strand, The, 101
Style, 47–9, 116
Subjects, 22–9
Submissions, 144, 152–5

Suspense, 64–5, 66–7, 159
Suspension of disbelief, 67–9

Talks, 135
Talleyrand, Charles Maurice de, 87
Teach Yourself Creative Writing, 30
Teenage books, 142
Television, 138, 162
Textbooks, 22, 104, 108
Themes, 23–4
Third person narrative, 63–4
Thomas, Dylan, 121
Through the Looking Glass, 40
Thurber, James, 75
Titles, 29, 150, 160
Topicality, 111, 160
Translations, 107–8
Typewriter ribbons, 13
Typewriters, 13–14

Underwriting, 61
Unities, the, 130–1
Unwin, Stanley, 160

Vanity publishing, 126, 157–8
Verbs, 42–3
Verse, 120, 122–4
Volume rights, 148

Way to Write, The, 47
West, Mae, 24, 25
What not to write, 74, 110–11
Wibberley, Mary, 14
Wilde, Oscar, 79
Willard, Barbara, 39, 43
Wilson, Colin, 78
Winter's Tale, The, 39
Woman's Hour, 135
Women's magazines, 101–2
Word counts, 51–3, 147
Word processors, 13, 14, 145
Words, 17, 38–55
Words, four-letter, 41–2, 129
Writer's block, 15–16
Writers' Circles, 9, 24, 26, 56, 145, 159, 164, 165
Writers' Guild of Great Britain, The, 164, 166–7
Writers' Summer School, 165
Writing habits, 14–15
Writing requirements, 13–14